C000054952

Villages of Banburyshire

including

Lark Rise to Candleford Green

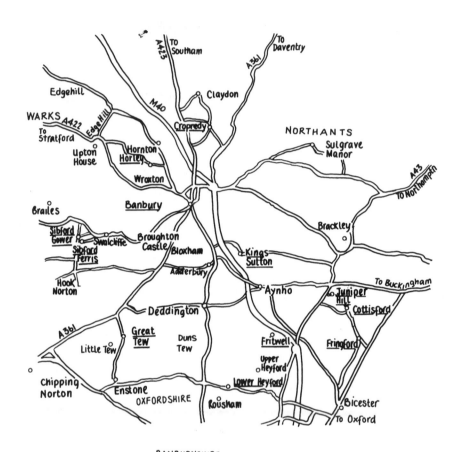

BANBURYSHIRE

The ten selected villages are underlined

Villages of Banburyshire

including

Lark Rise to Candleford Green

Martin Greenwood

Martin Greenwood

THE WYCHWOOD PRESS

Our books may be ordered from bookshops or (post free) from
The Wychwood Press, Alder House, Market Street, Charlbury, OX7 3PH
01608 811969

e-mail: wychwood@joncarpenter.co.uk

Credit card orders should be phoned or faxed to 01689 870437 or
01608 811969

Please send for our free catalogue

First published in 2006 by
The Wychwood Press
an imprint of Jon Carpenter Publishing
Alder House, Market Street, Charlbury, Oxfordshire OX7 3PH

The right of Martin Greenwood to be identified as author of this work has
been asserted in accordance with the Copyright, Design and Patents Act 1988

© Martin Greenwood

All rights reserved. No part of this publication may be reproduced, stored in a
retrieval system or transmitted in any form or by any means electronic,
mechanical, photocopying or otherwise without the prior permission in
writing of the publisher

ISBN 1 902279 24 7

Printed in England by The Cromwell Press, Trowbridge

Contents

Foreword and acknowledgements

'It seems inconceivable that there could be anything new to find in a place which we have been living in for a decade or more. We have become habituated and therefore blind.'[1]

'History with its flickering lamp stumbles along the trail of the past, trying to reconstruct its scenes, to revive its echoes, and kindle with pale gleams the passions of former days.'[2]

Over the past decade or more, I have been 'stumbling along the past' and 'trying to reconstruct its scenes' in lectures and village walks. There is so much to see and find in our villages, even if 'we have been living in (them) for a decade or more'. Recently, in revisiting my notes, I was amazed to find that I had guided walks round over twenty villages in this way, and this has inspired me to assemble this selection of village walks. All the villages are in Banbury's hinterland, a region once known informally as Banburyshire. Indeed, as recently as 1983, someone could write that 'The expression Banburyshire is still preserved, somewhat rebelliously, by Banburians wishing to irritate fellow countrymen, particularly those in the City of Oxford.'[3] I must state that it is not my intention to irritate those in the City of Oxford! I do believe, however, that there is some justification and merit in seeking to preserve the name of Banburyshire.

My hope and aim is to act as a lively and well-informed guide to each of the selected villages, rather than to provide a comprehensive history of them. Those who are interested can extend their research and examine the various sources in greater depth. If there is a particular focus in the book, it is on changes in village life in the nineteenth and twentieth centuries. As a resident of Fringford (Candleford Green), I have been particularly inspired by Lark Rise to Candleford, in which Flora Thompson writes so vividly about life in Oxfordshire villages in the late Victorian period. She was writing about an era when so many of our parents, grandparents or great-grandparents were growing up. In many families, memories and photographs have been handed down and it is a period to which many of us can relate easily.

While I would not claim to have unearthed much original information, I have spent many happy hours exploring these villages, examining a variety of records and sources, and talking to local residents, particularly the older ones. All sources have value, as someone wrote recently, and he added 'And by no means the least are the beliefs/legends of individuals and communities, 'true' or 'false'.[4] I heartily agree and I have much enjoyed listening to the legends. My walks have included a mixture of architectural, local, and social history, as I have attempted to present and explain some of the changes in village life. These changes have continued at an ever-faster pace in the last decade and this makes it all the more important that we preserve memories of the past. I hope that this selection may be of some interest to present and future generations who come to live in and visit these villages. I should emphasise that this selection of villages is entirely personal and random. As a result, I think that it serves to show the rich and varied character of the villages of Banburyshire.

I am very grateful to the residents of all the villages who have shared their memories and photographs with me. In particular, I must thank the following: Ray Cherry and Martin and Sue Lester of Cropredy, Mary Riley, formerly of Horley, John Allen, Jacqui Combes and Gwen Taylor of King's Sutton, Arnold and Ina Lamb of Sibford Ferris, and Eric Payne of Sibford Gower. I am also very grateful to Wafic Said and June Buck / Country Life Picture Library for allowing me to reproduce the photograph of the new Tusmore Park. I must also thank all those who have walked with me and contributed to the general enjoyment of numerous village walks. I am particularly indebted to those who have explored and already written or gathered material about some of these villages and allowed me to share their findings.

I would like to thank the following for their interest and support and for sharing their knowledge of Banburyshire: Brian Little, Graham and Jeremy Wilton at the *Four Shires* magazine, and Martin Allitt, at the Centre for Banbury Studies. Similarly, I must thank Malcolm Graham and the staff at the Centre for Oxfordshire Studies for their patience and assistance in answering my queries and for allowing me to use some photographs from the collections of the Oxfordshire County Council Photographic Archive (OCC). I would also like to thank the Greening Lamborn Trust for their generous grant towards the cost of reproducing these photographs. I am very grateful to Julie Barrett who has drawn the beautiful maps, and to Alec McNab for his rigorous reading of the text and suggesting improvements in many places. Finally, I am hugely indebted to Jon Carpenter for agreeing to publish this book.

Martin Greenwood
Fringford, January 2006

The Cattle Market in Cowfair, Banbury c.1878. Cattle were sold in the streets for the last time in 1931, when the dealers' market was transferred to Grimsbury (OCC).

Notes

1 Alain de Botton, *The Art of Travel* (2002), 147.
2 Winston Churchill, Eulogy on Neville Chamberlain, delivered at the Houses of Parliament on 13 November 1940; included in *Well-Remembered Friends* by Angela Huth (2004).
3 Martin Blinkhorn in Preface to *The Pathways of Banburyshire* by E. Walford (1900, revised 1983).
4 M.V. Roberts, '…history is about conjectures', *Local History News*, No.76. Summer 2005, 26.

Chapter 1

Banburyshire: myth or reality?

'The term 'BANBURYSHIRE', much used in the 1830s, was not just an affectation, for Banbury's economy was in many respects comparable with that of most county towns.'[1]

'The Shire'

'Banburyshire, Barsetshire, Edinburghshire, Hallamshire, Richmondshire, and Winchcombeshire'. How many of these shires were real counties? The last four were at various times but Anthony Trollope could write at the end of *The Last Chronicle of Barset*, '...to me Barset has been a real county,' and many would say the same of Banburyshire. Even in prehistoric and Roman times there was 'an intensive network of trackways' in the Banbury district, including Banbury Lane, which ran roughly from Northampton to Middleton Cheney. Indeed 'the frame of the area is set by a great triangle of Roman roads comprising the Fosse Way, Watling Street and Akeman Street'.[2] Later, Davis's map of 1794 clearly identified the Banbury area as the 1st District in the North Division of Oxfordshire. The southern limit of the District was on a line with Deddington, with the Chipping Norton and Bicester Districts further to the south.

Banburyshire may have been an informal term but the region is easily recognisable. Geographically, much of the region is the 'Red Lands', where local quarries have produced a golden brown stone used extensively in Banbury and neighbouring villages. This is also the rich, rust-coloured, corn-producing land, which the agricultural expert Arthur Young described in 1809 as 'the glory of the County, and adapted to every plant that can be trusted to it'.[3] There are also some obvious boundaries to the region. To the north, there is the steep Edgehill escarpment and to the south, the Buckingham-Aynho-Deddington road, which was the ancient boundary between Wessex and Mercia. To the east, Brackley is a natural limit and to the west, Swerford, Hook Norton, and the Sibfords, while Chipping Norton is clearly outside Banburyshire.

The Market Place, looking east, with carriers' carts c.1878 (OCC).

In the eighteenth century no less than seven turnpike roads linked Banbury with neighbouring towns. Communication depended on the stagecoach, the wagon and the village carrier with his horse-drawn cart. In 1778 a further big advance in communications came with the opening of the Coventry to Oxford Canal as far as Banbury. In particular, this meant cheaper coal, a better supply of raw materials and better distribution for finished goods. In 1790 the Banbury to Oxford stretch of the canal was opened. These advances led to significant increases in the population of Banbury and the surrounding villages during the nineteenth century. However, the populations of all the selected villages, except Fritwell, had peaked by 1871 and most of them by 1851 (see Table on p.16 below).

The term 'Banburyshire' was familiar in the late eighteenth and early nineteenth centuries, and was much used in the 1830s. In 1843 the extent of Banbury's hinterland and influence was well defined by the editor of the Banbury Guardian: 'To the 140 places within a circuit of ten miles it may be said to be a metropolis'.[4] In 1855, a map was published which specifically showed the ten-mile circuit around Banbury.[5] In recent times another map has been published 'of the area within a ten-mile radius of Banbury traditionally known as Banburyshire'.[6]

Banbury's influence extended well beyond this ten-mile circuit. Further afield, many countrymen sent orders to Banbury tradesmen through their weekly carriers or visited its annual fairs. In particular, crowds attended the annual Mop, or Hiring Fair, in October, when hiring was done on the street. A lady who died in 1956 aged 83 'remembered seeing farm workers waiting to be hired by farmers, and sealing the bargain with a shilling. She recalled there was a trial period of one month, after which if master and man did not get on, the man could come into a minor fair at Banbury (i.e. the Runaway Fair), and seek another master.'.[7] In other versions, when the labourers were hired, they 'were given a 'fastpenny' or 'earnest money', which they spent on ribbons with which to deck themselves, and enjoyed their freedom for the rest of the day.'[8]

The 1830s saw the passing of the Poor Law Amendment Act in 1834, and the establishment of a new Banbury 'Union', which was said to represent the greater part of the Banbury Region, and provide the only known political definition of the area. In addition to the Banbury borough, the new 'Union' consisted of 50 other parishes, 35 in Oxfordshire, 8 in Northamptonshire and 7 in Warwickshire. This is a further indication of how Banbury's influence transcended official county boundaries and how

The Market Place, looking west, c.1920. The cars, from left to right, are a Morris (c.1914), a rare French Delaunay Bellville (1908), and a Model T Ford (c.1911). The Delaunay Bellville had been the Tsar's favourite car! (OCC).

Edmund (T.E.) Tasker of Cropredy and Joseph Bates of Souldern at the 1908 Carriers' Annual Convention in Banbury. For well over a century these carriers' carts provided the only link to Banbury for some 140 villages (Martyn Lester).

its status was like that of a county town rather than just a successful market town.

The Carriers

By 1838, the 30 or so carriers named in Rusher's List of 1799 had grown to 208 carriers paying 465 visits per week to the town. The carriers were seen as the symbol of Banbury's prosperity. The town had many more carriers' services than county towns like Oxford, Newcastle and Shrewsbury, and only a few less than places like Nottingham, Leicester and Reading.[9] The carriers' routes show that Banbury's influence was felt in places as much as 20 miles distant. Most villagers had neither the time nor inclination to travel to town themselves as shoppers but carriers often fitted rough benches as seats for those who wanted to make the trip.[10] All the selected villages had carrier links with Banbury, at least on a weekly basis for the Thursday Market Day, although three of the villages were well over ten miles distant. In 1838, there were also 54 coaches leaving Banbury each week travelling to London, Birmingham, Coventry, Leicester and Cheltenham.

At this point, it is worth pausing to reflect on what the countryside around Banbury might have looked like on a market day in the high days of the 1830s. Early in the morning, from every village in the hinterland, there would have been a carrier or two, with his horse and cart, on the move to his chosen Banbury inn. Along the roads there would also have been great droves of cattle and sheep making the trek to the market. Each carrier might have been bringing dairy and horticultural produce to the shopkeepers, a passenger or two for a small fee, and some shopping lists and other errands for the villagers. It would have been a slow journey, with a number of stops along the way, taking perhaps three hours, for example, from the Sibfords. In the evening, when the carriers had completed their business and no doubt enjoyed some liquid refreshment and local gossip at their regular inn, there would have been another slow journey back with goods for their customers. The measured progress of all these carts and cattle would have been in stark contrast to today's traffic speeding to Banbury on the M40.

The Railway

The year 1836 marked the zenith of the stagecoach, before the arrival of the railway. By 1837 trains were running from London to Tring and travellers came on by coach to Banbury. In 1838 coaches ran to other points to connect up with the railways. In 1850 the railway reached Banbury, with the Buckinghamshire Railway beating the Great Western by a few months.[11] Locally, this had a particular effect on Lower Heyford, where the halt was built in 1850, and later on King's Sutton, where the station was built in 1872. Banbury, however, was never a major railway centre and the new railways of the 1870s did not bring it significant benefits. Indeed the carrying trade actually expanded in the 1870s and by 1881, 191 individual carriers were still making 438 journeys per week into the town.[12] By 1896, the number was down to 165 carriers paying 397 visits.

Plush-weaving[13]

Until the late eighteenth century, agriculture and weaving were the staple industries of Banbury, the latter since the Middle Ages. The surrounding parishes were largely dependent on agriculture, at least until the late nineteenth century, but there were also silk, linen and woollen weavers in many of them e.g. Horley, Hornton, Shutford, and the Sibfords. Weaving of plush cloth, earlier known as shag, had become established in the seventeenth century. By 1807, there were reckoned to be a thousand handloom weavers employed in the area. In the 1830s, the plush trade in Banbury was controlled by three firms, Gilletts, Baughen, and Harris, Banbury & Harris, with about 430 looms. Census returns of 1841 show the Banbury area having some 45% of all plush- weavers in England. The specialties in the district were shag plush, which was used for the seats of railway carriages, and Shutford plush, which was for the livery of Royal servants. Following the economic depression of 1839-42 the local industry declined. This was partly due to competition from plush-weavers in the north of England and partly to the growing importance of power looms. Both Gilletts and Harris gave up plush-making and in 1857 Baughens went bankrupt. By 1861 only 50-60 people were still employed in the plush industry. Cubitts, successors to Gilletts, were the last plush-maker in Banbury. They closed in 1909 but plush-making was carried on by the Wrenches of Shutford until 1948.

Nonconformity

In historians' terms, most of the selected villages have been 'open' rather than 'closed'. A closed village may be described as one where a squire or absentee landlord owns at least half the acreage e.g. Fringford and Great Tew, while an open village would have many small proprietors e.g. Cropredy and Fritwell. This is not an absolute distinction and there are obviously many other factors and intermediate cases.[14] One common characteristic of open villages is Nonconformity and Banburyshire has been a stronghold for Dissenters or Nonconformists over a long period. This has brought conflict to the region, particularly during the Civil War period, when Broughton Castle was the scene of the initial planning to overthrow Charles I. The region also witnessed the destructive sieges of Banbury and the battles at Edgehill and Cropredy, apart from numerous smaller skirmishes. In the 1851 religious census for Oxfordshire, the Banbury Registration District had by far the largest percentage (44.29%) of Dissenter sittings.[15] Most of the selected villages have had a strong dissenting or nonconformist element and in some cases still have, e.g. Fritwell and the Sibfords. This element has included Wesleyan and Primitive Methodists, Baptists, Independents, Quakers and Roman Catholics and a number of smaller splinter groups.

The Twentieth Century

Banbury's influence on the region has continued to the present day. Until the 1920s the carrier's cart was still providing the only link with the Banbury market for many villages, and there were still great droves of cattle and sheep making their way to the Market Place. However, this was

A Midland Red Bus at the old bus station in front of the Town Hall, 1920s. The carriers' carts were gradually replaced by buses in the 1920/30s (OCC).

increasingly inconvenient and the market was transferred to a syndicate of stock traders, Midland Marts Ltd., who moved to a new site in Grimsbury. The site was opened for auction sales in 1925. The move was a great success and by the 1960s Banbury was the largest stock-market in England. However, June 1998 saw the refusal of planning permission and the end of trading at Banbury Stockyard, although it is difficult to imagine Banbury without a stockyard. The 1920s and 1930s saw the gradual replacement of the carriers' carts by the omnibus, local taxis, and 'shar-rybangs' for communal outings or bringing tourists from the cities. 'The country bus was the motorized version of the old horse-and-cart village carrier, who simply modernized his existing business and became a busman.'[16] By 1950 the Banbury trade directory recorded only 16 carriers.

In 1943, this region was chosen out of all England for a systematic study and film of rural life under the title 'Twenty-Four Square Miles'. Although the chosen area did not cover the whole of Banburyshire, as defined above, it included Banbury and was bounded on the west by Hook Norton and the Sibfords, and on the south by Deddington. The film and report highlighted the extent of the decline in agriculture since the depressions of the late nineteenth century and the poor state of rural housing. It revealed that less than one-third of the working population was then working on the land (the current figure is less than 2%). It also showed the dire need for post-war reconstruction. In most Banburyshire

Banburyshire Populations 1801-1991

Village	1801	1851	1871	1901	1931	1951	1991 (Note 4)
Cropredy	470	**596**	520	436	425	452	666
Fritwell	396	514	552	452	468	497	530
Lower Heyford	346	605	**625**	494	415	398	478
Horley	269	392	338	247	209	213	296
King's Sutton	1,021	**1,335**	1,319	1,101	990	1,146	2,082
Sibford Ferris	213	**350**	308	255	332	194	291
Sibford Gower	397	**549**	449	394	301	374	462
Great Tew	402	**541**	504	334	334	284	147
Cottisford (Note 3)	106	263	**327**	161	169	154	140
Fringford	252	357	**479**	335	268	331	537
Town							
Banbury	4,070	8,793	11,768	**13,026**	13,998	18,916	38,154
Bicester	1,946	3,054	3,328	3,023	3,110	4,171	20,244
Brackley	1,515	2,277	2,331	2,487	2,097	2,531	9,115
Chipping Norton	2,200	3,368	4,092	3,780	3,499	3,878	5,351
Oxford	12,279	27,843	31,404	**49,386**	80,539	98,684	124,058
Oxfordshire	111,977	170,434	177,960	**181,149**	209,784	275,808	547,584

Notes

1 **Bold type** = peak populations 1801-1901

2 Other dates for peak populations 1801-1901

    1841 Horley 425   1881 Chipping Norton 4,222; Fritwell 560

    1891 Bicester 3,343; Brackley 2,614

3 Cottisford includes Juniper Hill.

4 The table does not include figures from the most recent 2001 Census, as comparable parish populations are not available.

villages, electricity and mains water did not arrive until the late 1950s or early 1960s nor new housing until around the same time.

In 1974, when Cherwell District Council was formed, it might have been expected to cover the old Banburyshire. Surprisingly, it also included Bicester and its environs, which have little if anything in common with Banbury. More recently, Banbury's influence has been revived by the opening of the M40 motorway in 1991. This has made Banbury an ideal business centre and one of the lowest areas for unemployment in the whole country. 'The second largest town in the county has always been conscious of its individuality and has never lost an opportunity to express it.'[17] South Oxfordshire, the old Berkshire, has always seemed remote, with Henley more distant than Birmingham. The new regional assembly in Guildford is likely to seem even more remote. Perhaps, at some future date, the inevitable reversal of centralisation may yet bring authority back to Banbury and reality to Banburyshire. For the present, whether the shire is myth or reality, let us simply enjoy the rich heritage and variety of these Banburyshire villages.

Notes

1   Barrie Trinder, *Victorian Banbury* (1982), 16.
2   Brian Little, *Banbury – A History* (2003), 1.
3   Mary Jessup, *A History of Oxfordshire* (1975), 15.
4   *Banbury Guardian*, 6 July, 1843, quoted by Barrie Trinder, *Victorian Banbury* (1982), 16.
5   Stones's map 'Ten Miles round Banbury' (1855).
6   Graham Nottingham based on a 1985 original map by G.G. Walker (1999).
7   *Cake and Cockhorse*, Autumn 1969, 73.
8   M. Lovett Turner, *Stories in Stones*, included in *Countryside Mood* (ed. R. Harman) (1943), 128.
9   Barrie Trinder, *Victorian Banbury*, 82.
10   Valerie Porter, *English Villagers – Life in the Countryside* (1992),
11   Ted Clark, *Banbury History and Guide* (1992), 41-3.
12   Barrie Trinder, *Banbury – A History*, 147.
13   Vera Hodgkins and Christine Bloxham, *Banbury and Shutford Plush* (reprinted 2004).
14   Kate Tiller, *English Local History* (1992), 221-2, quoting Dennis Mills.
15   Kate Tiller, *Church and Chapel in Oxfordshire 1851*, xli.
16   Valerie Porter, *English Villagers*, 57.
17   Martin Blinkhorn in Preface to *The Pathways of Banburyshire* by E. Walford (1900, revised 1983).

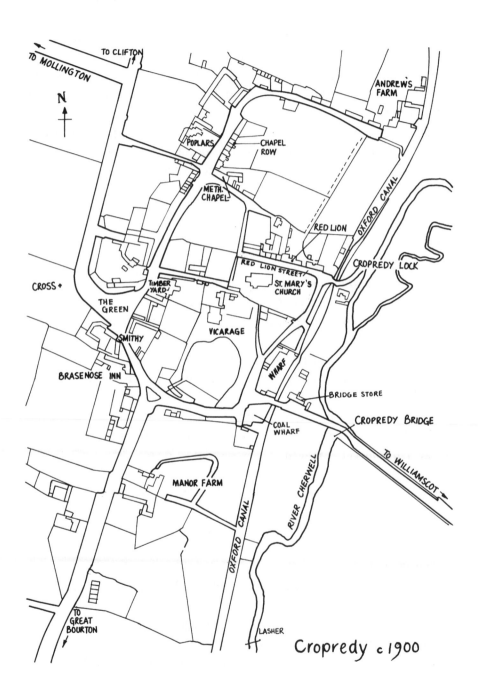

TO CLIFTON

TO MOLLINGTON

N

ANDREW'S
FARM

POPLARS

CHAPEL
ROW

METH.
CHAPEL

RED LION

OXFORD CANAL

CROSS +

RED LION STREET

CROPREDY LOCK

THE
GREEN

TIMBER
YARD

ST. MARY'S
CHURCH

VICARAGE

SMITHY

WHARF

BRASENOSE INN

BRIDGE STORE

CROPREDY BRIDGE

COAL
WHARF

TO WILLIAMSCOT

MANOR FARM

RIVER CHERWELL

OXFORD CANAL

TO
GREAT
BOURTON

LASHER

Cropredy c 1900

Chapter 2

Cropredy

Cropredy is four miles north of Banbury and can be reached off the A361 Daventry road or the A423 Southam road through Great Bourton. The Banbury-Southam road is the old Roman Via Regia or Regalis, and later the Broadway, which was turnpiked 1755-1878. The Banbury-Daventry road, the Banbury Way, was turnpiked 1765-1871. The name Cropredy seems to derive from a combination of 'crop' meaning a hump or hill and 'ridig' meaning a small stream. A ditched causeway from the ford crosses the meadows to the higher ground, and a southbound causeway is now Station Road. Cropredy, like Lower Heyford, became a junction of road, rail and the canal.

In the mid-seventeenth century, the village and the wider parish were 'very populous'. The wider parish included Wardington, Prescote, Mollington, and Great and Little Bourton. In 1801, the population of Cropredy alone was 470. It reached a peak of 596 in 1851 before declining to 436 in 1901. In 1961, it was still only 459 but had risen to 666 by 1991. Under the Enclosure Award of 1775, the main beneficiaries were Sir William Boothby (982 acres), the Bishop (253acres), and Brasenose College (190acres). The Boothbys were the leading family from 1618 to 1788. They owned the manor from 1680 to 1788 but there was no dominant squire. In 1776, when the Boothby finances collapsed, John Chamberlin, the famous Commissioner of Enclosures, bought three Boothby farms. It may have been at this point that the village was sold to Brasenose College, Oxford. Following enclosure, outlying farms were built to replace the ones in the village.

In 1851, there were 11 farmers, with 6 farming over 100 acres. The farming was mainly pasture, so that the agricultural depression in the 1870s was not so disastrous as in other villages. 27 traders were listed, including 4 masons and 4 carpenters. In 1899, there were still 9 farmers and 24 traders. By 1939, there were still 9 farms but only one over 100 acres, and 15 traders. The main village families have been the Wyatts, who were farriers, the Gardners, who were collar makers in the seventeenth and eighteenth centuries, the Lamberts, who were builders, farmers, and coal merchants and also ran the Red Lion, the Taskers, who were carriers in the nineteenth and twentieth centuries, and the Cherrys, who have been well-known builders for over 130 years, as well as farmers, carriers, coal merchants, and masons. There were carrier links with Banbury from 1796, generally three times a week. From the 1870s, William Cherry was going to the Unicorn, 20 Market Place and one of the Taskers to the Flying Horse (now called 'Ye Olde Auctioneer'), 44 Parsons Street. Edmund Tasker was still going there twice a week in 1928.

Farmers, like the Wyatts, Lamberts and Eagles, were prosperous in the sixteenth and seventeenth centuries and built good-size houses. 1670 to 1700 was a busy period for building in the village and the village houses of this period are mainly two-storey, ironstone with Welsh slate roofs, brick stacks and casement windows. There was an early brick works locally c.1790 after the canal was opened to Oxford, possibly along the canal near the Mill.

The Canal

The Coventry-Oxford canal opened as far as Banbury in 1778. By 1784, there was a company wharfinger based in Cropredy and a coal wharf had been built. By then a number of farmers were also coal dealers. In 1790, the Banbury – Oxford stretch of the canal was opened and the price of coal in Oxford dropped by 50%. In 1830, the Cropredy tolls of £1,175 were over one-quarter of the Banbury ones. By then six or seven express fly-boats were going weekly in each direction. It was the peak time for them, just before the railway age, carrying merchandise and passengers.

'These express boats ran to a timetable using relays of horses and double crews, carrying merchandise and parcels setting down and picking up at wharves along the line with priority over all other traffic and permission to work all through the night.'[1] 1842 saw the peak, with over 9000 boats going over the Claydon summit, just north of Cropredy. By 1845 decline had set in with the arrival of the railway. Later, specially designed boats carried by-products of the Banbury Gas Works such as tar, ammonia, water and coke. These were in regular use until the Works closed in 1958.

The recent increase in narrow-boating for pleasure has meant that Cropredy is still an important stopover on the canal before the climb through the locks to the Claydon summit. This has been helped by the major repairs and improvements to the canal and towpath carried out by British Waterways. Other attractions bringing tourists to Cropredy are its

Civil War connection, through the Battle of Cropredy Bridge, and The Fairport Convention, the folk festival, which is held every summer.

The Railway

The Banbury-Leamington section of the Great Western line was opened in 1852, and Cropredy station, built in the same year, was also included on the Oxford-Rugby line. The East & West Junction Railway, from Blisworth to Worcester, ran north of Claydon, and the Great Central line ran from Woodford Halse to Banbury, via Chacombe Halt. In the 1920s the train to Banbury was too expensive at 3d for most people, so many used a cart or walked. All these railway lines were closed between 1952 and 1966.

The Battle of Cropredy Bridge, 29 June 1644[2]

In early June 1644, Charles I had slipped out of Oxford and led the Earl of Essex on a wild-goose chase through the Cotswolds. Essex did not cooperate with his generals like Willam Waller and finally gave up and marched south-west to relieve Lyme Regis, which was under siege by Prince Maurice. Waller continued the chase, while Charles, reinforced with some 10,000 men, looked for a chance to take the offensive. Waller had also received reinforcements from Warwick and Coventry, and was at Kineton by 26 June. Parliament was again worried that Charles might be able to march on London if he defeated Waller.

Waller was enticed from a fine position on Crouch Hill (south west of Banbury) by Charles marching away towards Daventry. He shadowed the Royalists via the Southam road, with the two forces marching parallel about a mile apart, separated by the River Cherwell. Waller took the Great Bourton road, leading to the Cropredy bridge, which the Royalists rushed to protect with a party of dragoons.

The Royalist column became invitingly strung-out, so Waller sent troops to the bridge, under Lt. Gen. John Middleton, and himself crossed the river at Slat Mill in an effort to split the column and trap the rear half. Tactically it was brilliant but it went horribly wrong. The Earl of Cleveland met Middleton's attack and the Earl of Northampton repelled Waller's advance. A second assault by Middleton was beaten back to the bridge by Cleveland, with help from Lord Bernard Stuart, and they captured the bulk of the Parliamentary guns. Waller then drew back to Great Bourton, leaving detachments to hold the bridge and the ford at Slat Mill. Charles drew up his forces on the Daventry road at Williamscot. He managed to overrun the ford but the bridge held out.

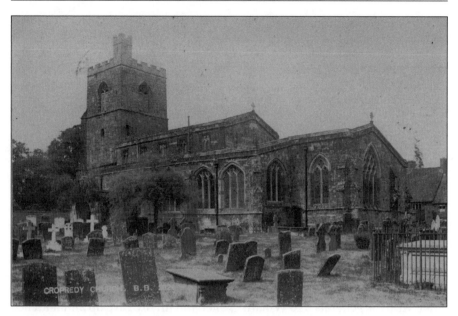

St Mary's Church and churchyard, postcard c.1906 (Martyn Lester).

We may conclude that the day belonged to Charles and it did guarantee Oxford's safety. However, it was really only a sideshow, with all the drama in the north at the battle of Marston Moor on 2 July. Charles, needing fresh troops and provisions, left Waller in Great Bourton and withdrew towards Evesham, where on 3 July he heard of Rupert's defeat at Marston Moor. Waller and Browne, who had been at Buckingham, linked up at Towcester. However, the London and Home Counties troops were impatient to go home. They thought that the war must be over and they deserted in droves. So Waller returned to London, abandoning the remains of his army at Abingdon.

We start our walk at St Mary's Church (GR 469468).

ST MARY'S CHURCH is mainly thirteenth and fourteenth century and is dominated by the wonderful perpendicular arches. The lower part of the wall of the south aisle has been dated as early as 1050, and may form part of an earlier church. Set in the wall are two arched sepulchral recesses which are thought to be the tombs of father and son – both called Simon de Cropredy, who c.1200 lived at the Manor House (now the Old Manor House). The font in the north aisle also dates from this period.

Co-operative shop in Red Lion Street with the Manager and delivery boy outside, 1920s (Martyn Lester).

13th century: in the south aisle, in front of the fifteenth-century Chapel of St Fremund, there is a fine old parish chest with three locks, one for the vicar and one each for the two churchwardens.

14th century: the nave, with its fine perpendicular arches leading up to the great chancel arch, and the choir arches, all date from early in this period. Above the chancel arch are the remains of a doom wall painting, which was probably hidden during Puritan times. There are also some remains of wall paintings in the north aisle.

15th century: the brass eagle lectern is a very rare example of pre-Reformation work of this century, and the only surviving one in England outside Oxford. The lectern was hidden in the river on the eve of the Battle of Cropredy Bridge in June 1644. When the lectern was recovered after the Civil War, one of the three brass lions which formed the feet was missing. The eagle was so discoloured by the water that the replacement foot was made in bronze not brass as you can see today. The beak of the eagle may have been used to collect Peter's Pence, a tax paid to Rome. Coins were removed from a slot in the tail, which is now closed.

17th century: the pulpit is reputedly carved from a Cropredy oak tree, and bears the date 1619. Above the pulpit are the remains of a doorway to the Rood Screen. Sadly Cropredy's collection of Civil War armour was stolen from the church but there is still a display case with replica armour in it.

19th century: the north aisle, which had been extended in the fifteenth century to form the North Chapel, was partitioned in 1825 to form the choir vestry. This now contains the organ which was built in 1860 and enlarged in 1922. Note the two-light window above to provide a view from the priest's room. The fine clock, dated 1831, was built by John Moore & Son of Clerkenwell to replace the original clock, which was there pre-1512.

Churchyard: note the old sundial and the lantern turret on the tower, which was built in two stages in the fifteenth century. The 1877 date on the drainpipes is the date of a major reconstruction. On the right of the south gate, there is a blocked entrance to the Old Vicarage, and opposite there are some richly carved seventeenth-century gravestones.

Hello Passage (or Hellhole) runs from the south gate. The passage wall was built in 1814 by the vicar, John Ballard (1811-51).

Walk back past the west door of the church into Red Lion Street.

Red Lion Street, formerly Cheapside.

The cottages in this street are mainly seventeenth- and eighteenth-
century. The street was a tradesmen's row with tailors, saddlers, coal
merchants, masons, carpenters, plumbers and glaziers living and
working here. April Cottage, opposite the iron gates of the churchyard, may be the oldest cottage, where a small dwelling had been built
in the garden by 1681. Calverton House, next door, was the home of
the Gardener Brothers, painters and glaziers, who had their workshop
on the left. No.2 has been owned by at least five generations of the
Jennings family who still live here. There used to be a sweetshop just
up from the Red Lion, and, just below it, there was a nineteenth-
century shoemaker's cottage, which later became the Co-op Stores.

The RED LION was licensed in 1753 but it was probably here in the
time of the Civil War. After 1778, it was a stopover for horses used by
the canal boats. A skeleton was found under a paving stone during
alterations by William Hadland of Clattercote in the early nineteenth
century. The Old Malt House next door was never a malthouse.

HOLTWOOD, formerly the old mill barn, at the bottom of the street;
was converted in the early nineteenth century into a saddler's house,
with a new brick front and sash windows.

The OLD MILL: Lock Cottage and the canal lock were built in the yard
of the old mill when the canal was opened in 1778. Across the bridge,
the two Riverside Cottages, with brick lintels, are on the site of the old
millpond. The road leads to Prescote Manor Farm, where Dick
Crossman, the famous Labour politician and diarist, used to live.

At Domesday in 1086, there were 5 mills in the parish, and in 1968 there
were still 5 mill cuts on the Cherwell. In 1774 the mill was worked by
Michael Pratt. William Hadland acquired it c.1824 and made great
additions. However, in 1831 he built a new mill at the southern end of
the village, when he built Bourton House nearby. In 1851, the Pratt
family was still working it but in 1892 it was ruined by a fire.

Cross the bridge and join the tow-path southwards.

The Tow-path

On the right before the bridge, there used to be a toll-house at the
narrowest point of the canal, where an oak boom was used to stop the
boats for payment. There was also a corn granary and a wharf. There
were still three wharves c.1900.

The wharf on the Oxford Canal, with the Old Navigation Inn building, 1920s. A toll-bar used to be put across the narrowest point (OCC).

The NAVIGATION INN (originally called 'at the Navigation Wharf')
was here on the right from 1778 to 1796. Previously, three generations
of the Read family lived here. These may have been the first sash
windows and hip roof in Cropredy.

HOLMLEIGH, off Round Bottom, behind the inn, was a malthouse,
run by Walker, a farmer, c.1800. There was a Dame school here in the
1830s until the old Dame died. The Hodgsons then opened a Dame
school opposite. Holmleigh became the home of Robert Smith, who
built the National School in 1854.

At the canal bridge, walk up the steps to join the road and turn left.

THE BRIDGE STORE, which dates from the late eighteenth century,
was built by Walker of Holmleigh, After the canal opened in 1778, he
became a coal dealer like a number of local farmers, and owned
several coal barges.

CROPREDY BRIDGE, beyond the Store, is first mentioned in 1314
when there were repairs to the bridge; there were further repairs in
1691 and 1780. From 1884 to 1886 the bridge was rebuilt and widened
by Thomas Cherry. In 1937, reconstruction revealed remains of the
earlier bridge. There is a notice on the bridge commemorating the
Civil War and the battle: 'From Civil War Good Lord Deliver Us. The

Site of the Battle of Cropredy Bridge 29th June, 1644.' The Cropredy Sports Ground is just beyond the bridge.

Retrace your steps over the canal bridge.

THE OLD COAL WHARF, on the left, was built after the canal opened in 1778 and was in operation by 1784. Note the inlet where boats could be repaired. John Foley has done considerable restoration work on the wharf. On the right of the entrance, where there used to be a weighbridge, is the old clerk's office. Apparently the original weigh-bridge was too small for the regular carts, which had to be propped up in an elaborate fashion before they could be weighed!

THE PLANTATION area was so named because the vicar John Ballard (1811-51) planted trees opposite Brasenose Inn and down the south side of the Green towards the canal.

PLANTATION COTTAGE, on the left, used to be two cottages, dating from 1677 and 1717. There is a Victorian pigsty in the garden. Edmund Tasker, the village carrier, used to live here and keep his cart in the coach house which is attached to the house.

Opposite, on the corner of Station Road, three cottages were bought by the Copes of Hanwell and altered c.1800; No.6 is still called Copes Cottage. Nos. 6 and 8 seem to be the original buildings, while Nos. 2 and 4 must have been added later.

Turn left up Station Road.

CHERRY FIELDS, on the right, formerly Blue Gate Close: Thomas Cherry and Sons used to have their builders yard here after Thomas Cherry founded the building firm in 1875. He built the Methodist Chapel in 1881 and in 1884 to 1886 he rebuilt the bridge. The firm oper-ated very successfully from here until 2000, when it moved to Great Tew. It is now run by Stephen Cherry, the fifth generation of builders.[3]

THE OLD MANOR, formerly Brasenose Manor Farm, on the left, was once moated and was substantially built by 1593. A 1540 lease tells of providing lodging for the visiting Principal & scholars of Brasenose College, who attended the Manor Court here. The oldest part is the north end and the oldest wall is on the river garden side, where there is a rare six-light window on the ground floor. By 1627, the remainder of the farm had been added by the Woodroffes.

The Wyatts lived here from 1668 to 1787. In 1693, Thomas Wyatt (1668-1710), who lived here with his nine children, made substantial alterations, copying the new style of wooden transomed windows at the south end. He also added the south wing (note 'WTM 1693' on the south gable) with a parlour or hall. In 1718, a new wing was added with a living-room and the original building became a service wing. The manor was owned by the Boothbys until 1788, when their finances collapsed and Brasenose College acquired it.

In the nineteenth century there was dairy and beef farming here on about 90 acres. In 1888, the College water supply arrived and in 1910 an inside water-closet was installed upstairs for Mrs Francis. In 1924, Mrs Longbotham requested a bathroom from the College but the plans were never used. In 1937/38, electricity arrived. In 1939, training courses for Landgirls were held here and a further request was made for a bathroom 'even if of the most elementary nature'. The College regretted that 'more pressing matters make it necessary for me to postpone this for the present'!

SPRINGFIELDS, formerly Station Farm and Watkins Farm, was leased by the Grisolds in 1706 and it was their home for 150 years. They were then tenants of Brasenose Manor Farm. Springfields was rebuilt in 1888 when George Smith, a Liberal and Chapel man, was the tenant. There is a Victorian letterbox by the gate, placed there to be near the old station, which opened in 1852 and was closed in 1956.

BRASENOSE COTTAGES, on the left beyond the Old Manor, are six Victorian cottages built by the College. Gardner Godson, whose bakery was in Church Lane, used to live here.

The CHURCH OF ENGLAND PRIMARY SCHOOL, at the end of Station Road on the left, was built by Robert Smith in 1854 as a National School for Cropredy and Bourton. The road by the school leads down to the 1831 mill.

Retrace your steps to the Green.

The Green

The BRASENOSE INN was originally three copyhold cottages, one of them an early smithy. In 1665, Richard Denzie was living here, when it was a single dwelling with three stone fireplaces. Local church courts were held here. Later, the Anker family were licensed vict-uallers here for over 150 years. At the rear there used to be a stable block with a large loft above.

The 'Brazen Nose' was Brasenose College's bronze sanctuary knocker, placed on the College gate in Oxford in 1279. It was moved to Stamford, Lincolnshire in 1330, where it remained until 1890. The early fourteenth century saw turbulent times and the College was seeking a more peaceful site for studying. The College and the 'Brazen Nose' returned to Oxford in 1890.

CONSTONE, like other older cottages in the village, was built before the canal opened i.e. pre-1778.

The CUP and SAUCER, at the top of the present Green: before the bridge was built, the Green used to stretch from here to the ford. There are many tales as to the origin of the Cup and Saucer but there seems no doubt that it was used as a medieval 'Preaching Cross' by the monks from nearby Clattercote Priory. The shaft was cemented into the base when it was moved here from its original position in the fields towards Oxhay Farm.

PEARTREE HOUSE, formerly Fairview, was a seventeenth-century manor house, which included Wingsmore and Seymour Cottages. The west front is that of a later saddlers/carpenters. The Lamberts owned and altered the house in the early nineteenth century, when brick became available. It was once a large farmhouse with a yard and hovels behind, a natural place for a farm on the Green before the 1775 Enclosure.

Walk past the Green Scene Coffee Shop to Church Lane on the right. The Green Scene is a very old building where Ray Cherry's family used to live.

BEECH HOUSE, formerly Poultry Farm, on the left next to the new vicarage behind the high beech hedge, was an early farm site and home of the Eagle family. In the nineteenth century the Anker family lived here. They were carriers and chapmen i.e. pedlars, and they used to have a poultry farm behind. The village pond used to be next door, where three modern cottages now stand.

Church Lane

THE OLD FORGE, on the corner opposite the new Vicarage, used to be the Post Office. This was the home of Frank Sumner who ran the business of blacksmith and wheelwright in the buildings across the yard. The Post Office was run by his daughter, Connie. Across the

Church Lane and St Mary's Church tower, 1930/40s (Martyn Lester).

road was the cobbler's shop and, next door, an earlier Post Office run
by the Harris family.

The OLD BAKEHOUSE: note the original sign on an old bread paddle,
and the loft into which they used to hoist 280lb sacks of flour! The old
fireplace and bread oven still survive inside. John Allitt was the baker
and butcher here in Victorian times. He took on the business from his
uncle, Thomas Checkley, who in 1814 brought the first brick to
Church Lane. Checkley used to attend the Banbury market at the
Unicorn every Thursday, c.1811 to 1836. In the first half of the last
century, William Godson and his son, Gardner, were the bakers, and
William lived next door to the bakery.

The CHURCH ROOMS, with a datestone 'JA 1887', were built in 1887
for John Allitt. He presented them to the village as a reading-room.

The cottages on the south side were copyhold, built on the original Green,
while those on the north side are much earlier and originally built of
timber. All the south-side properties had a cowshed with a hayloft
above, as they had common rights of pasture up to the time of
Enclosure in 1775. The old vicarage used to be on the right and the old
building by the church's west gate was originally the stable for his pony.

Walk through the churchyard into Red Lion Street and continue up the street.

The Wesleyan Methodist Chapel and Chapel Row, early 1900s. The Chapel was built by Thomas Cherry in 1881 (Martyn Lester).

HONEYPLECK, formerly Home Farm, on the corner, is brick-faced and was altered about sixty years ago. It was once The Rose and Crown Inn, which was licensed from 1763 to 1786 and run by William Hemmings. Pleck means 'waste or common land' and Honeypleck is the name of one of the fields which once belonged to the property.

The POST OFFICE, behind the Methodist Chapel, was originally a stable, converted into a chapel in 1822. The entrance must have been on the gable-end, where there is a 'small bricked-in circle which could have been either a small window or, more probably, a plaque'.[4] In 1851, attendance here was 73 in the afternoon and 90 in the evening. In 1881, the chapel was altered to a dwelling house by Thomas Cherry, when he received it as part-payment for building the new chapel.

The METHODIST CHAPEL was built in 1881 on land belonging to Edward Shirley, who had his wheelwright's yard and pond here. Thomas Cherry built it for £700 and he also received the old chapel in part-payment. The buttresses were added later. The new chapel is an impressive size and could accommodate more than twice the number of the old chapel. One visiting missionary went by the lovely name of William Norwell Zackarrat Ploughshare! The chapel is still very well supported in the community.

CROMWELL COTTAGE, across the road, is on the site of three old
cottages which were demolished when Keith Handley built the new
cottage in 1977 (note his new datestone). The original datestone 'BGH
1694' refers to George and Hester Blago.

STONESFIELD, which used to be an old thatched barn, was also rebuilt
by Keith Handley into two cottages and is now one.

The DOWER HOUSE, formerly Lyndhurst, on the corner of Newscut
Lane, was built c.1840 by the Eagles of Poplar Farm for Mrs Eagles,
Sr. Watts the weavers worked their looms here for generations. Is
Newscut Lane perhaps related to 'scutching', which was the treatment
of flax by retting or beating it?

Chapel Row / Creampot Lane

CHAPEL ROW COTTAGES include five seventeenth-century cottages,
which began as one farmhouse and barn under a single thatched roof,
and another separate cottage on the south end. The three on the north
end date from c.1700. No.3 was a double-fronted house and has a
1632 datestone. There is an old through-passage between Nos. 7 and 8
which once led to Mr Pargeter's shoe shop. The Old Posthouse (No.9)
was once the Post Office. Note the blue Ratley paving bricks outside
all these cottages, which were put down all over the village in the
1840s to ease walking.

EAGLES, formerly Poplar Farm, which dates from 1580, was the home
of the Eagles family. There is an original doorway and mouldings.
The Tapleys did extensive renovation to the house and to the barn,
which also dates from 1580 and has an old dovecote window. There is
an insurance fire-mark on the south side. The original central core of
the house runs east-west and is best seen from the garden. The north
wing was added in the early eighteenth century. In 1825, a brick-faced
wing was added on the north-west. On the south side a second storey
and chimney were added but they were too heavy and it all fell down!
A 1910 photograph shows a conservatory on the south side and there
are still signs of its roofline.

DORMERS was originally part of Poplar Farm. The old stables at the
rear, which are in line with Eagles's barn, have an original floor of
blue Ratley bricks. There is also evidence of old pigsties in front of the
stables. The old brew-house on the left probably dates from the eighteenth century and has a bread oven, copper (an iron cooking or
laundry boiler), and old fire-back, which were preserved in the 1990s

conversion. The builder of the brew-house was a brick-maker and some of his original bricks have been reused.

POPLAR COTTAGES was originally a row of four cottages provided for the farm workers on Poplar Farm. This was one of the four major farms in the village and at various times it was occupied by Lamberts, Watts, Hazlewoods, and more Eagles.

THE HOLLIES was a barn which was rebuilt in 1846 and turned into three cottages by William Elkington (a 'WE' datestone above the front porch is just visible).

Beyond some new cottages are the OLD STONE COTTAGE and READS HOUSE. A three-bay barn was built here in the 1680s for the Watts and converted after the 1775 Enclosure into eight cottages. Below Reads House, the 1900 OS map shows a row of five cottages and another four cottages on the site of North End.

ANDREW'S FARM, at the end of the lane, was mainly built in 1821 and the date 'TA1821' can be seen on a drainpipe by the back door. The earliest house dated from c.1550 and was crossways to the present one. The McDougalls from Prescote Manor used to own it and, behind the farm, there is an old right of way and bridge across the canal to the Manor.

Walk through Creampot Close and New Place. The Close was possibly so named because it was close to the Old Manor House (now No.11 Red Lion Street). Rejoin Red Lion Street and retrace your steps to the church.

Notes

1   Joseph Boughey, *Hadfield's British Canals* (revised 1994), 147.
2   David Clark, *Battlefield Walks – The Midlands* (1993), 111-120.
3   Ray Cherry, *Memories of Cropredy* (2005).
4   Pauline Ashbridge, *Village Chapels* (2004), 49.

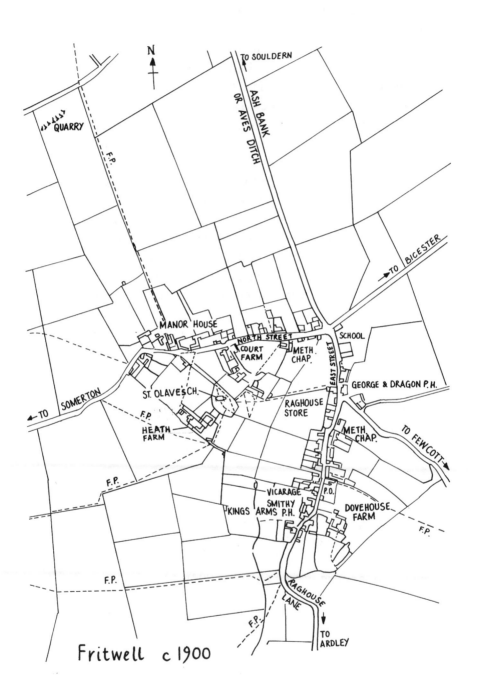

Fritwell c 1900

Chapter 3

Fritwell

Fritwell is some two miles north of Baynards Green and junction 10 of the M40, and nine miles from Banbury. The name means 'wishing well or spring' and probably refers to an old spring near the church which is generally accepted as the source of the River Ouse. In Saxon times, there were two settlements, each with a manor house and separated by open fields. The church was built midway between the two settlements early in the eleventh century, probably on the site of an earlier church. After the Norman Conquest in 1066, William I granted the lands of 'Fertewelle' to Bishop Odo, who in turn gave them to Wadard, his steward and chief huntsman. He is distinguished by name on the Bayeux Tapestry.

This early history has contributed to the interesting shape of the village, with two manors, the former 'De Lisle Manor' on North Street, and 'Ormond Manor' on East Street where Lodge Farm now stands. There were two village greens and, unusually, the old rectory on East Street was detached from the church. From early times the village is remarkable for the number of houses and cottages not forming part of the property of the manors.

As early as the 1660s, in addition to eight substantial farmhouses paying hearth tax, there were eight other houses, including The Hollies, The Limes, and Pitts Farm which still stand today. In 1754, there were twenty-nine 40s. freeholders registered for the General Election, second only to Bicester in the Ploughley Hundred. In the eighteenth century, there were some 66 houses and much rebuilding took place. The plain dignity of some of these houses is still evident on East Street. Enclosure took place in 1807, when the principal awards were to William Fermor and the late J.Kilby (715 acres) and the Revd W. S. Willes (488 acres). The vicar was also relieved of the duty to provide a bull and boar for baiting. William Fermor was a member of the Catholic family who owned the neighbouring Tusmore estate.

In 1801, the population was 396. Unusually for the area, which was very dependent on agriculture, the village did not suffer a sharp decline during the agricultural depressions of the 1870s and 1880s. Indeed the population rose from 514 in 1851 to a peak of 560 in 1891. In 1852, 'Fritwell in the Elms', as it was known, was described as 'expensive and respectable',[1] and it was noted for its numerous craftsmen and tradesmen. Today, it is more likely to be referred to as 'Frittle'. Trade directories show a remarkable consistency from 1852 to 1928 in the number of farmers (6) and trades (18). More detailed examination of the Census Returns reveals a much higher number of trades and occupations: 93 in 1851 and 62 in 1891. The 1852 numbers include 18 lacemakers who had all gone by 1891 as lacemaking moved to commercial centres like Nottingham. By 1901, the population had declined to 452 and it was only 468 in 1931. In 1991 it was still only 530 but there has been some new building since then.

In terms of family continuity, the Allens ran the laundry at The Limes from 1886 to 1948, Mrs Eliza Golder kept a shop with the Post Office c.1899 to the 1930s and the Bennett, Tebby, and White families were all involved in various occupations for well over 50 years. The Dew family and Dews Stores warrant a special mention below. Carrier links with Banbury started in 1832, with Robert Boddington going to the Waggon and Horses (now Banbury Cross) in the Shambles/Butchers' Row on Thursdays. John Bennett took over in 1864 and he continued the link with the Waggon and Horses for over fifty years. He had similar links with Bicester on Fridays. Wilfred White succeeded him and he was still the carrier in 1939, although by 1928 the village also had an omnibus proprietor, Walter Kingston.

The lack of a dominant squire or vicar in the nineteenth century seems to have contributed to the rise of Methodism in the village. By 1851 there was a small chapel, probably in Southfield Lane, off East Street, with a congregation of nearly 100. As the curate commented in 1854 'The parish in a religious point of view has been thoroughly neglected. Dissenters took the opportunity to establish themselves'.[2] By 1878 the Methodists were said to form about one-third of the population and a new chapel had been built on East Street. In 1892 the new North Street Chapel and Temperance Hall was completed, and it is still in active use. That is not to say that Fritwell was by any means a typical 'open' village. Most of the Methodists seem to have been happy to enjoy the variety and novelty of church and chapel, while on occasion the Anglicans might attend chapel.[3]

No guide to Fritwell would be complete without a mention of Frank Dew and his family. In 1886, he was responsible for the building of the huge Raghouse Store on East Street, which was reputed to be the largest village store in England. His businesses prospered and he became very much a leading local figure. Indeed, you might almost call him the local squire, and in 1916 his son George was excused military service, as being 'too important to the local economy'! Frank Dew was also a key member of the local Methodist community. He had his own chapel, he was reputed to employ only Methodists, he expected his staff to go to chapel and he was a driving force in the building of the new chapel on North Street.

Today the village still has a thriving primary school, a shop and two pubs.

We begin our walk at the church, just across from the Manor (GR 524293).

ST OLAVE'S CHURCH is first recorded in 1150, although the dedication to St Olaf or Olave, the patron saint and king of Norway who died in 1030, suggests an earlier dedication in the 11th century. The church was rebuilt in 1166 by Ralph Foliot, tenant of the Ormond Manor on East Street. He also gave land for the manse by the King's Head. This was possibly so far from the church because the land round the church belonged to the De Lisle Manor on North Street.

12th century: the superb Norman doorways, nave arcades and the arch on the north wall of the chancel survive from this period. In the south porch, the doorway is of special interest, with the remarkable carving on the Norman arch and a fine tympanum showing two beasts feeding on each side of the Tree of Knowledge.

13th century: the south aisle and the tower were added, when the chancel was rebuilt. The holy stoup is also from this period.

14th century: the north aisle was added with decorated windows.

15th century: extensive work probably included building the former clerestory with square-headed windows, adding new windows in the aisles and a battlemented top to the tower.

19th century: by 1854, the church was 'in the most disgraceful possible condition and unsafe to minister in'.[4] The Revd Samuel Yorke, with the architect G.E. Street, undertook major restoration. This included rebuilding the tower with a pyramid roof, replacing the nave roof, building a larger chancel and moving the Norman arch to the north chancel wall, replacing the old oak pews and removing the western gallery. Street is also credited with the fine stone pulpit, the cross, and reredos behind the high altar and the altar rails. Bishop Wilberforce reopened the restored church in 1865.

The immense organ loft, organ and vestry screen were made up from
Jacobean woodwork in 1901 following a bequest from Hannah
Hopcroft. The impressive lych-gate dates from 1922, the gift of Lord
Simon and his wife, who lived in the De Lisle Manor from 1911 to
1932. There is a memorial plaque here to the five men from the
village who died in the Great War.

THE GREEN: as you leave the church, note the classic layout of the
Green surrounded by the church, the manor opposite and a number
of seventeenth-century farms: Heath Farm on the left, where George
Dew lived, Court Farm on the right, Wodards next to the manor, and
Home Farm beyond.

Turn left towards the West End.

HEATHLANDS, on the left, has a datestone on the gable-end from the
1920s 'FA192?'. The house may have been built by one of the
numerous Allens.

WHEATCROFT, formerly The Bear and the Wheatsheaf Inn, closed
c.1964. The iron frame for the inn sign is still attached to the outer
wall. The T-shaped building probably dates from the seventeenth
century. The Bear Inn was kept by John Bennett, the carrier, and then
Mrs Ann Bennett c.1847 to 1915.

Round the corner on the right, there is one of the Fritwell springs, now
hardly visible. Some of the locals can recall a pond and a well here.
Homelea opposite was built in 1932 on the site of some old cottages.

Turn back and walk along North Street.

North Street

TOWN WELL END and NEW HOME FARM, on the left, are recent
developments. The land was originally all part of HOME FARM,
which probably dates from the seventeenth century.

The three cottages beyond Home Farm, including MILLER'S
WHISTLE and SUNNYSIDE, date from the eighteenth century. The
porches were added later.

WODARDS, formerly Manor Farmhouse or Home Farm, probably
dates from the late seventeenth century, when the Manor House was
extended, but parts may be earlier. In the 1920s, Lord Simon restored

the house for his daughters and modernised the old farmyard and cottages but they never lived here. When he married again in 1926, they went to live in India, some say to avoid the second Lady Simon! However, they may not have wished to live next door to their father, who is described in the Dictionary of National Biography as 'A man of outstanding cerebral talents with scant popular appeal'! Colonel Hodson's father rented the property from him and then bought it in 1931. Colonel Hodson and his wife lived here until the late 1990s.

DE LISLE MANOR HOUSE: the central core, with the mullion windows, probably dates from the late sixteenth century. In the early seventeenth century, Edward Yorke (whose initials EY are over the main fireplace) rebuilt the house in the E-shape with the three-tier porch and sundial. There was once a powder room above the porch. Inside there are a number of stone-carved fireplaces, oak panelling, a fine staircase, and a state bedroom from this period. There are also mullion windows and a tiny square window from the same period on the roadside wall of the stable. The present owners are doing some major refurbishment to the house and stables.

The manor has had a colourful history, of which the following gives a flavour:

17th century: in 1651 Colonel Sandys, the Royalist owner, was not allowed out of Oxfordshire or into Worcestershire, where the family still occupy their home in Ombersley, without a special licence. By 1661 another Royalist, Sir Samuel Danvers, was living here. He owned another manor at Culworth, Northamptonshire, where he had received Charles I on 27 June 1644, before the Battle of Cropredy Bridge. During his stay, a member of the family, Pope Danvers, was killed by a Mr Jackman in a duel at the manor. In 1683, an extension was built at the rear.

18th century: in 1712 Sir Edward Longueville, a prominent Catholic, was imprisoned by his younger brother, George, in a room off the long attic above the drawing room; it had a fireplace but no windows and it was probably a 'priest's hole'. In 1718, George fell from his horse at Bicester Races and died on 19 August. His brother Edward died a week later.

In 1729, the manor passed to the Wake family from Northamptonshire. In 1735, another tragedy hit the manor, when Sir Baldwin Wake killed his son, Baldwin, after a card game. Charles, the brother, took

BY DIRECTION OF THE RT. HON. SIR JOHN SIMON, G.C.S.I., M.P.

FRITWELL MANOR, OXFORDSHIRE

Station, Bicester (G.W. Ry.), one hour Paddington, also Brackley (L. & N.E. Ry.) from Marylebone.

THE BEAUTIFUL AND HISTORICAL TUDOR MANOR HOUSE (1599–1611) stands on gravel and stone soil, 420ft. above sea level, faces due south, and is built of stone with stonesfield roof, and contains inner and outer halls, four-five reception rooms, thirteen-fourteen bed and dressing rooms, five bathrooms, complete offices, etc. *Telephone, electric light, central heating, ample water and modern drainage.* Stabling, garage, chauffeur and gardener's cottages, guest house, assembly hall ; old-world gardens and grounds and paddock. *Hunting with the Bicester and golf at Tadmarton Heath.* The Property extends to about

TEN ACRES.

If desired, the Home Farm, comprising 119 ACRES, can be purchased.

Further particulars of the Agents, JOHN D. WOOD & Co., 23, Berkeley Square, London, W. 1. (Mayfair 6341.)

Notice of Sale of the Manor by Lord Simon in 1932 (OCC).

the blame and went abroad to live. In 1747, Sir Baldwin confessed on his death-bed and Charles returned to inherit the title but he never returned to Fritwell.

19th century: there was no dominant squire or family living in the manor during this period. The Willes family owned it from 1770 to 1863, although they were only occasional residents after 1802. They often let the manor for short periods during the hunting season. The quality of the Bicester Hunt was well known and in 1857 the district was described as being 'studded with Gentlemen's Seats and Hunting Boxes, affording society of the most agreeable kind'.[5] A noted tenant for the hunting seasons between 1813 and 1819 was the 'amateur

pedestrian' Captain Barclay Allardice (1779-1854), who had walked
1000 miles in 1000 hours in 1811. He became notorious for bringing
coloured prize-fighters, like Cribb and Molyneux, to fight bouts in the
hall with local men on Sunday afternoons.

After the Willes sold the manor in 1863, the vicars, Samuel York (1863-
76) and Reginald Remington (1876-93), lived here. Remington
carried out extensive repairs, removing most of the attic floor on the
east side and with it probably the 'priest's hole', scene of the
Longueville tragedy. From 1893 to 1906 Thomas Garner, the famous
church architect, partner of G. F. Bodley and pupil of Gilbert Scott,
lived here. He obtained papal dispensation to have mass said in the
manor.

20th century: in 1911, Sir John Allsebrook, later Lord Simon and Lord
Chancellor, bought the manor which 'was still a museum piece'. He
carried out extensive restoration in 1921 (there is a datestone at the
rear), including the new west wing. It is notable for its poor taste and
design and use of unsuitable Yorkshire stone. During the Second
World War the building was used as a rest home for wounded pilots.

COURT FARM HOUSE, formerly Hickock's Farm, opposite the
Manor, dates from the seventeenth century but was remodelled and
extended c.1800. The barn, which has now been converted, was built
at that time. The last Hickock died in 1638 and the Court family lived
here from then until the nineteenth century. The L-shaped farmhouse
has stone mullion windows and some blocked windows, possibly to
avoid window tax. This tax was imposed in 1696 to succeed the
hearth tax. It was not abolished until 1851, although houses with
fewer than eight windows were exempted in 1825.

GARDENER'S COTTAGE, which has just been re-thatched, and
HAWTINS COTTAGE, on the left, were both part of the Manor's
property. Note the view of the water-tower behind, which was built
by Lord Simon.

THE LITTLE MANOR was built by Lord Simon for his mother in the
1920s. It was later a guest-house and then a rest-house for the
wounded during the Second World War. Simon also built the 'manor
barn' in the garden for village entertainments.

MAY'S HOUSE, on the left, is an old farmhouse dating from the seventeenth or eighteenth century. The datestone 'HB1835', on the front
wall of the east wing, refers to Henry Borton, who added this part.

The WESLEYAN REFORM METHODIST CHAPEL /

The Wesleyan Reform Methodist Chapel/Temperance Hall in North Street, in 1906. Frank Dew and Enos Cox had it built in 1892 (OCC).

TEMPERANCE HALL was built in 1892, as stated on the date-stone. Frank Dew built it on land donated by him, with money from his partner, Enos Cox. There was already a chapel on East Street and Frank Dew had another one in his store. However, by 1878 about one-third of the population i.e.150 to 200, was Nonconformist and there was clearly a real demand for a new chapel. There does not seem to have been any conflict between the East Street and North Street chapels. The chapel remains in active use by the Wesleyan Reform Methodists.

BERRYBANK HOUSE, on the left, is a well-built eighteenth-century house, with a modern rear extension. The old house was the original Fullers Farm, where one of Frank Dew's sons lived. In the 1990s, the rear part, which had been the cow byre, was modernised and an upper storey was added.

FULLERS FARM, on the corner, was the site of the barn and other outbuildings for the original farm. The new house was built in the 1990s. The pond opposite, which may have been used for washing carts, has been restored.

Turn right at the crossroads into East Street. Note the plain dignity of many of the eighteenth-century houses on this street.

The CHURCH OF ENGLAND PRIMARY SCHOOL: a National

school and a mistress's house on the right of the school were built here in 1872 for £700 on glebe land donated by the Revd Samuel York. There had been a variety of schools in the village prior to this one, run by Catholics, Dissenters and the Church of England. In 1808, some children were being taught by a Dissenter who had been a Catholic. Relaxed relations between the different faiths seem to have been the norm. The school continues to prosper with some 160 children. The mistress's house was sold c.1990 for private use and recently the trustees have sold the old school building for a private dwelling. The school is now housed in new buildings, and is building some new classrooms and an Early Years block.

THE GEORGE AND DRAGON was originally built in the seventeenth and eighteenth centuries but has been extensively modernised.

THE RAGHOUSE STORE, possibly the largest village store in England at one time, was built in 1885 for £1000 by Frank Dew with money from Enos Cox (datestone on the gable). The name derives from an original Rag House, which was set up on the south side of the village between the sixteenth and seventeenth centuries to supply rags to the Deddington paper mill. The lane past the King's Head to

'Dew's Groceries, Haberdashery and Ironmongery Store' on East Street in 1904. It was said to have been the largest village store in England (OCC).

The Wesleyan Methodist Chapel on East Street, built c.1827, 1920s (OCC).

the Heyfords used to be called 'Raggus Lane'. 'Dew's Groceries, Haberdashery and Ironmongery', was a 'wholesale and retail provider' of almost everything. At its peak, there were 22 employees and numerous horse-drawn carts delivering to all the neighbouring villages. On the rear wall, you can still see the blocked doors on each floor, where the hand-winch was used to load and unload the carts. The store closed in the 1970s and the whole building has been converted recently into luxury apartments.

It appears that Dew employed only Methodists and there seems to have been a strong network of Methodist craftsmen and tradesmen in the village, many of them living around the store. On Sundays, he was a preacher on the Methodist circuit but, for the rest of the week, he was clearly a very shrewd businessman. It was said, for example, that he or one of his staff, was likely to be a new mother's first visitor after the midwife, with offers of a pram, cot, and all the essentials for the new baby!

Dew lived next door in the house with a porch (now Crail House), which seems to date from the eighteenth or early nineteenth century. Like the store, the house has been modernised recently but the interior still has traces of the earlier building. Dew had his own chapel here. To the south, the whole building was used for storage, with an entrance for sugar (for making preserves) and a grain store. Dew even

East Street looking north towards Dew's Store in 1904 (OCC).

had to rent the disused chapel on East Street for extra storage. He
also bought the three cottages on the opposite corner for a bakery but
he died before he could complete the project. Behind the store, there
used to be an old brick water-tower.

CHAPEL HOUSE, on the left, was probably built c.1827 by the Mores,
who may have lived near the village shop. In the 1851 religious
census, attendance of 68 in the afternoon and 84 in the evening was
recorded by John Tebby, Steward, Carpenter. The chapel was closed
in the 1920s and used for storage by Dew. It is now a private
dwelling. In 1868 there was an interesting service here, when 'The
Chapel was crowded to excess' to hear a Miss Ghostley preach.
George Dew, churchwarden at Lower Heyford, admitted that 'Her
sermon was very good & to the point. But respecting whether women
ought to preach I know not what to say'! The vicar had warned his
church congregation against it. However, 'Many who, before, had
never been to Fritwell Chapel went today.'[6] It was clearly regarded as
entertainment for all, whether you were Church or Chapel, just as the
rededication of St Olave's by Bishop Wilberforce had been in 1865.
There were many Dissenters, 'who sometimes go to one place, some-

times to another' and in 1866 'only 8 Dissenters who attend Chapel and never enter Church'.[7]

THE HOMESTEAD (No.62), on the right, is a fine large eighteenth-century house, with a walled garden behind. Note the long closes behind it and the other houses here.

LORNA VILLAS, on the right, was built in 1912 for Thomas Simons, in spite of Sir John Simon's understandable objections. The building is more in keeping with south coast suburbia! It replaced three thatched cottages which had burned down. A butcher and baker (Henry Scott) and a wheelwright/undertaker had lived there. It seems likely that they were all Methodists.

BEAR COTTAGE (Nos.39 & 41), opposite, used to be two thatched cottages. They and Lilac Cottage (No.37) are all listed eighteenth-century cottages.

G.B.WRIGHTON AND SONS, on the left, is the only shop open today but there were many others from Victorian times at least until the Second World War.

BAY TREE COTTAGE (No.76), on the right: note the gable-end and the old newel staircase on the south side. Such staircases are a feature of Oxfordshire cottages and they were not built much after 1750.

THE HOLLIES, on the right, dates from 1636. Note the faded date-stone 'NK1636', which probably refers to a Kilby. The family owned properties on either side and was resident in the village from the 1630s to 1841. There were still holly trees here in the 1920s. The house has been restored in authentic fashion in the last decade and includes an Elizabethan-style knot garden.

SOUTHFIELD LANE, on the left: at the end there is a very small cottage, now enlarged, which may have been the original Methodist meeting room.

ST OLAVE'S, on the right next to the vicarage, was once church property. In the late eighteenth century, Jennings, a noted clockmaker, lived here. Apparently he lowered the ground floor to allow room for the large grandfather clocks. There is still an old cottage behind.

The OLD VICARAGE is on the site of the original manse. The southern wing, with two ground floor rooms and three bedrooms, is sixteenth-century; the remainder is seventeenth-century. In the 1920s, there were large gardens and a tennis court. The blacksmith's forge and cottage and a barn used to be next door. The forge was still operating after the Second World War.

THE POUND, which was an enclosure maintained by the manor or vestry to confine stray animals, used to be opposite the Vicarage and next to the old walled garden of Lodge Farm. The old wall still runs down to the road to the right of No.63.

LODGE FARM, formerly Dovehouse Farm, is on the site of Ormond's Manor House, later known as Ormondes Court. Note the good site for a manor house, on high ground with a water supply. In the seventeenth century, the Fermors of Tusmore purchased the farm and leased it to Samuel Cox, who married Alice Kilby of Souldern. They were both Catholics.

The older core of the present house dates from 1750 or earlier. The newer part, at right angles to the old house, was added c.1870. An earlier drive used to go up to the front door. The old dairy and barn have now been converted. The dovecote used to be straight at the end of the drive, where the concrete slab for it remains. You can still see the walled garden and the old pond, which has been enlarged.

RAGHOUSE or 'RAGGUS' LANE, the old name for the road to the Heyfords, runs from this point.

THE KING'S HEAD dates from the seventeenth century and was certainly licensed by 1735, like the George and Dragon and the Wheatsheaf. Daniel and Thomas Tebby were the landlords for over fifty years from c.1847, at a time when the Tebby family were Methodists. Presumably they were not Temperance men! Jack Hearn, who was the landlord in the 1920s, was also a shoemaker, ran a dairy and kept bees.

THE LIMES dates from the seventeenth century. Note the attic dormers, the stone-slate roof, the brick chimney shafts, and the spiral newel staircase in a square projection on the inn side. There is also an old tether for the horses. The front door is an unusual hinged one.

The LAUNDRY used to be in the shed behind The Limes. The original metal shed has been recently replaced by a wooden one. The Allen family ran the laundry here from 1886 to 1948, employing some ten people and doing laundry for a number of the local villages. The drying was done at the bottom of the garden. The laundry was modernised in the 1920s, when a new ironer came from one of the P&O liners. Some of the new equipment was said possibly to have been bought at the Wembley Exhibition of 1924. The Allens also bought their first motor vehicle then for £126, a Tin Lizzie Ford T van, which was specially painted in primrose yellow.

There were only three other laundries in the area, the Bennett brothers in

Oxford and Banbury and one at Gawcott House, near Buckingham. The Allens had contracts with most of the big houses for washing sheets and stiff collars, 300 collars every three days at 1d each! In the 1930s, they had contracts with the camps at Upper Heyford and Bicester. Eight ladies used to work in the laundry, with three of them living-in prior to 1914. Later, they all arrived in for work by 8.30am, three from Souldern, three from Fewcott, and two from Fritwell. Richard Allen recalled that their wages were c.6d. per hour.

THE FARM, formerly Pitts Farm, has a datestone 'IW1637' on the roadside wall. This probably refers to one of the Wise family who lived in the village from this period until the mid-nineteenth century. The north-south block probably dates from the nineteenth century, when the Pitts, who were Quakers, were living here. They were coal merchants and had a dairy on the north end, at least until 1928. They used to collect coal and milk from Somerton station. Three old cottages opposite have now disappeared but their old 'hovels' or outhouses survive.

The last two cottages opposite are seventeenth-century and one of them has a very worn 1657 datestone. Between the late nineteenth and early twentieth centuries, Jesse James, the pig-sticker, used to live in the last one. He used to charge half a crown per pig, in the days when the pig was so vital to a family's food supply.

Further down the lane, there used to be navvies' huts when they were building the rail tunnel in 1902.

Retrace your steps to Lorna Villas and take the footpath back to the church.

Notes

1   *Kelly's Directory*, Oxon 1864.
2   E.P. Baker (ed.), *Bishop Wilberforce's Visitation returns for the Archdeaconry of Oxford*, 1854.
3   M.W. Greenwood, *Parishes, Parsons and Persuasions* (1997), 48.
4   Bishop Wilberforce's Visitation returns, 1854.
5   J.C. Blomfield, *Fritwell* (1893), 85.
6   Pamela Horn (ed.), *The early diaries of George James Dew (1846-1928)* (1986), 67.
7   Oxford Diocesan Papers, d.179 & d.332.

Chapter 4

Lower Heyford

Lower Heyford, on the B4030 road from Bicester to Enstone, is some ten miles from Banbury and includes the hamlet of Caulcott. It has been called 'The Jewel of the Cherwell Valley'. It is bounded on the west by the river Cherwell and on the east by the Romano-British earthwork, Aves Ditch. Heyford probably means 'ford' strengthened with stakes called 'stoke' or 'haia', forming a rough hedge – hence Haiforde, 'the hedge-forde'. There was also a ford at Upper Heyford which is 20 feet higher. The two fords allowed settlers to cross to the markets in Steeple Aston and Steeple Barton. Because of the easy access to water and the fords, the site has been settled since the sixth century. In the fourteenth century, the village was called Heyford Purcell. This name appears on Plot's map of 1677 and was still widely used in the 1800s. The village is fortunate in having been mapped in considerable detail by Thomas Langdon in 1606.

The Portway, a major Roman road, runs close to the village and a coin from the Emperor Constantine's time (early fourth century) was found in the churchyard in 1941. The neighbouring hamlet of Caulcott had a Roman villa. At Domesday there were two mills and two fisheries. By the early 1600s, Lower Heyford had been sold to Corpus Christi College, Oxford. The Enclosure Award was made in 1802, with the largest awards going to Clement Cottrell-Dormer of Rousham (280 acres), Benjamin Churchill (177 acres), and the Revd William Filmer (c.90 acres). By 1850, the village had become a junction of road, river, railway, and canal. In 1790, the Heyford section of the Oxford Canal was completed. In 1793, the Bicester-Enstone road became a turnpike crossing the Heyford Bridge, and in 1850 the GWR railway arrived. Competition from the railway led to decline in road traffic and in 1877 the turnpikes were taken down and the toll-houses sold.

It is not surprising that, as Lower Heyford became a local centre for canal and rail trade, the population soared. In 1742, the population was

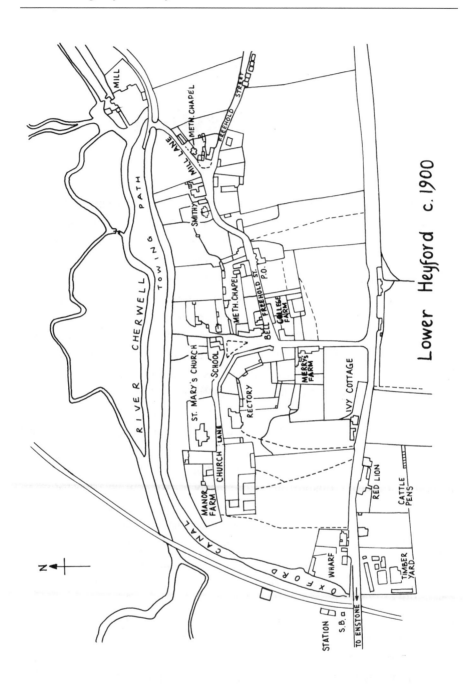

Lower Heyford c. 1900

215, including three pubs. By 1801, the population was 346, and by 1871 it reached a peak of 625. By 1845, a corn market had been started, and there were six cattle and sheep fairs and an agricultural show. By the 1880s, the village's fortunes were declining, and cattle and sheep sales were no longer held at regular fairs after 1889. By 1901, the population had fallen to 494. By 1951, this had declined further to 398 and in 1991 it was no more than 478. In 1876, 6 farmers and 14 trades were listed and in 1920 the numbers were similar. Carrier links with Banbury, which are mostly recorded under Upper Heyford, started in 1832. From 1843 the main link was with the Catherine Wheel in Cow Fair. From 1884 into the 1920s, Walter Boddington was the local carrier, going there on Mondays and Thursdays.

No account of Lower Heyford would be complete without some mention of the Dew family, who 'left a considerable mark on the life of Lower Heyford for almost a century and a half'.[1] This family is not to be confused with the Dews of Fritwell. George Dew (1844-1928), in particular, put the village on the map with his diaries. They start in 1862 and cover his early years and then his service as relieving officer for the poor. He was a real busybody, whose other activities included inspector of canal boats for Bicester Rural District Council and registrar of births and deaths, and he was always writing to the local papers.[2]

From 1906 to 1936 Lower Heyford was a centre for the arts, with a series of classical concerts and readings given in the village and at Steeple Aston, promoted by Reginald Lennard, son of the rector. As a young man, the conductor Adrian Boult was a regular weekend visitor to the Lennard household. The charge was 1d. per concert and 112 of them were given over 30 years. On 13 January, 1928, George Dew recorded that 'The aerodrome staff came to Upper Heyford aerodrome on Jan.3rd. Aeroplanes ever since flying noisily over us'.[3] The Base has had, and continues to have, considerable influence on the area, although the Americans left in the 1990s. A final decision on how to develop the site has yet to be taken. There are fears that it may involve a very large number of new houses, with an enormous impact on the local infrastructure.

The Canal

In 1778, the section of the canal to Banbury was completed. This led to a halving of the coal price in Oxford and Banbury, and it was "a great boon" to Lower Heyford and its neighbourhood.[4] Coal came south from the Midland coalfields, corn and grain went north to Birmingham, wool to Leicester and Kidderminster and barley to the Dudley brewers. In 1790, the Oxford section of the canal was completed and the wharf and the canal bridge were built. In 1852, Gardners trade directory records 'Excellent wharf on the canal, belonging to Mr Richard Coggins, so that the town affords abundant facilities for the transit of passengers and agricultural produce.'

The Railway

In 1850, the Oxford to Banbury branch of the GWR opened and the Lower Heyford Halt, one of the three original intermediate stations, was built by September 1850. The Halt employed a Station Master and six porters. This did not lead immediately to cheap travel but it did bring in cheap goods and materials e.g. for building. Cheap excursions to Weymouth and other seaside resorts and to London exhibitions did not come much before 1900. Local resident, Nellie Stockford, who died recently aged 106, recalled the annual outing to the seaside, getting up at 3am for the 4am train to Weymouth and returning after midnight. Others recall the start of the summer holidays for the Birmingham factories, when some twenty packed trains would come through in convoy to the south coast – all on time to the minute!

We start our walk at St Mary's Church, down Church Lane from the Market Place (GR 485249).

ST MARY'S CHURCH: the first church was a Saxon foundation
c.1057, of which nothing remains. The earliest work in the present
church is thirteenth-century. The following are some of its notable
features:
13th century: the chancel is pre-1220, and the lancet window by the
altar and the piscina near the porch date from this period.
14th century: the church seems to have been almost entirely rebuilt in
this period, probably pre-1350, as it was in a 'ruinous state' by 1338.
The chancel was reconstructed, the east window and other chancel
windows were added; also a timber roof and a small door in the
north aisle.
15th century: the clerestory, tower, and the stairs to the foot of the bell-
chamber were erected and the aisles were raised. Later, the south
porch and sundial (now replaced) were added, with the rood-stair
and a very fine rood-screen.
19th century: the church was restored in 1848 and 1868. The east
window is by C.E.Kempe, with his distinctive wheatsheaf signature.
You can also see some of his glass in the churches at Steeple Aston
and Aynho.

— July 7916. —

George James Dew, Registrar of Births & Deaths of the Bletchington District from 1870 – 1923. Clerk to the Lower Heyford Parish Council.

George James Dew, Registrar of Births & Deaths, July 1916 (Roger Bowen)

Other interesting items include:

a) A mid-twelfth-century chest for collecting money for the Crusades,
b) A medieval window, on the left as you enter, made from pieces collected from the churchyard by George Dew,
c) The vestry window, which has a lozenge with the Corpus Christi College badge of a pelican, with the initials TG, those of Thomas Greenway (rector 1563-71). It was moved from the rectory during rebuilding in the nineteenth century.

The Rectors[5]

Some of the rectors warrant special mention. Thomas Greenway (1563-71), ex-Master of Corpus Christi College, left the College after 'trouble with the ladies'. He brought two of them to Lower Heyford and was said to consort with 'infamous women'! The glebe then was over 1000 acres and Greenway built a new rectory. Thomas Cole (1600-46), an eccentric, was said to have been overcome by 'a great sadness of spirit', and between 1630 and 1637 entered his own burial in the church registers on eleven occasions!

Thomas Butler (1646-51), an army preacher, was alleged to 'keep strumpets' in Deddington, where he lived, and to preach in 'coat and Sworde'. John Dod (1651-62) resided here but did not once administer the sacrament to his parishioners, 'alledging that they were not fit for it'. Charles Fort (1866-68), a 'saintly character', rebuilt the rectory, restored the church and built the school.

The Manors

The Bruce and Merry families held the two main estates in the sixteenth and seventeenth centuries. In 1533, both manors were sold to Corpus Christi College but leased back by the two families until the eighteenth century. In 1765, the Cottrell-Dormers of Rousham acquired the lease of the Bruce estate, and in 1787 the lease of the Merry estate.

HEYFORD HOUSE, opposite the Church, was formerly the Rectory. In 1569, the east side was built by Thomas Greenway but there may be some older parts. The house fell into disrepair during the Civil War but by 1679 is said to have eight or nine bays. In 1731, the north wing was built by Thomas Leigh. In 1867, Charles Fort undertook serious rebuilding, pulling down the south side and most of the old parts. The lower cross-wing, to the left of the main nineteenth-century range, is on the site of the original house. There is a large walled garden behind, probably eighteenth- or early nineteenth-century.

CHURCH COTTAGE, next door, is early eighteenth-century, as is MANOR COTTAGE (No.16), on the right with a twentieth-century porch. Both were altered in the nineteenth century.

BRUCE MANOR, at the end of the lane, has a 1669 datestone on the west side, with the initials 'W.E.B.' (William and Elizabeth Bruce). The house has been rebuilt into an L-shape, with two storeys, an attic dormer and a seventeenth-century three-light window with a moulded wooden frame. This complex house has some earlier parts and at least three buildings seem to be involved. There may have been a dairy on the front where there is now a kitchen.

Take the footpath past the Old Coachhouse, which has been converted, and cross the field with the canal and the narrow boats on your right. There is a good view of the Old Coachhouse as you look back. Pass the walled garden of Manor Farm House and turn left at the main road.

There are three early eighteenth-century houses across the road, which were once the Red Lion Inn:

a) DARVILLE HOUSE, with a three-window bowfront, was formerly the public bars. At the rear is an eighteenth-century wing linked to an earlier beer store.

b) DARVILLE COTTAGE

c) OLD BARN COTTAGE was converted from an outbuilding range, and has an extension at the east end, now DARVILLE LODGE.

The inn is first mentioned in 1784 but it may have been one of three licensed in 1735. Boatmen used to hold their meetings here, and it was very well placed for the turnpike (1793), canal (1778-90) and the railway (1850). Benjamin Coggins was the publican in 1852. By 1876, he had been succeeded by his son Richard who was a corn and coal merchant and had been the wharfinger. The Bowling Green is opposite.

Walk back down towards the bridge.

THE BEECH HOUSE, on the left, is probably eighteenth-century, with a later addition at the rear and an early twentieth-century porch.

MANOR FARM HOUSE, opposite, has a walled garden behind. The east end of the house is eighteenth century or earlier. The lower end was added in 1898, when the path through the property was closed.

CANAL COTTAGE is the early nineteenth-century wharf manager's house. There used to be stables across from the house, with a weigh-bridge between them. The Bourne family were the wharf managers in the 1840s, and later carpenters and undertakers. They used to make coffins on the south side of the bridge. Heyford Wharf is still extremely busy with the hiring of narrow boats and all the passing trade. The railway station is immediately opposite.

The Long Bridge and Turnpike

The first mention of the bridge is in 1255. It was the first crossing of the river north of Oxford, and the arches at the east end date from the late thirteenth century. In 1793, the Bicester-Enstone road was turn-piked and two toll-gates were erected, one to the south-west near Rousham and another at the turn of the road to Caulcott. By 1840, the bridge was in ruins, and the county became liable for its upkeep after suing the parish and losing the case! In 1842, it was repaired for £209. The bridge is one of the places where people used to come to 'gongoozle' i.e. to stand and stare at the canal boats and the boat people.

Rousham Park

Walk to the far end of the bridge and causeway for a fine view of Rousham Park on the left. The house was built c.1635 for Sir Robert Dormer and it is still the home of the Cottrell-Dormers. The bridge formed an important feature in the landscape of Rousham, which was designed c.1740 by William Kent.

Walk under the bridge to inspect the old arches and see where the coal wharves used to be on the far side; then follow the tow-path north to Mill Lane.

The Tow-path

Note the narrow point on the canal just north of the wharf. It was here that they 'weighed' the boats with a bamboo pole measuring the height (depth) of the four corners to calculate the total weight and therefore the charge. There were also holes here to insert a board to block and drain the canal.

STATION ROAD, LOWER HEYFORD.

Above: Station Road with the old Red Lion on the left, postcard early 1900s (David Dare)
Below: The canal wharf and railway station looking towards St Mary's Church, 1983 (OCC).

As you walk on, note the gardens running down to the river and views of Bruce Manor and the church; also look for the site of Grantham's Wharf, off the Market Place, which was used for shipping timber and coal. There were seven wharves on this stretch of the canal, including one for the White Horse Inn. On the left, note the River Cherwell and Broadhead Meadow which was the subject of a long dispute with Steeple Aston.

Turn right at the swing-bridge.

THE MILL, on the left, is partly seventeenth-century, with some late eighteenth- and early nineteenth-century alterations and additions. It has been operated in living memory, with two mill-wheels and two water channels, one for grain, the other for hemp. Hemp was grown in Lower Heyford for rope and stout fabrics. In 1858, new machinery was installed, with four pairs of stones, but the flow drove only two at once.

MILL BRIDGE: huge carts used to go over the old swing-bridge, which dated from c.1790, although this bridge is the third or fourth replacement. Children used to raise the bridge for the boats and hope to get a penny. Nellie Stockford recalled that in 1957 some of them dropped it on a Mr Compton and nearly hit his boat!

Mill Lane

CHERWELL HOUSE, on the right, is on the site of Dorothy Dew's retirement home. She was the schoolmistress for over fifty years. On her retirement in 1939, she lived here with Mrs Busby until her death aged 94. There used to be a swivel summer-house from the 1924 Wembley Exhibition in her garden but it was burned down.

MILL LANE COTTAGE, on the left, was the home of Mrs Clist, who used to raise the swing-bridge for the boats. Nellie Stockford lived there earlier, when the family used to provide a stopover for the boatmen and mangers for three of their horses.

THE OLD METHODIST CHAPEL, on the left, was built in 1904 and the foundation stone says 'G.C.Banbury JP, July 7 1904'. It replaced the first chapel next to Forge House. Two old cottages were removed to make space for it. In the 1940s and 1950s it was used as a Baptist Chapel by the US forces from the Upper Heyford Base.

Methodism took root in Lower Heyford from the early nineteenth century. Thomas Rose, the miller, built the first chapel by Forge House, and the 1851 religious census records a Wesleyan Methodist congregation of 50 in the morning. Methodism was stronger in neighbouring Caulcott and Upper Heyford.

WHEELWRIGHT'S COTTAGE, on the corner, has a well in the middle of it, which has been preserved.

FREEHOLD STREET, to the left, has been owned by Corpus Christi College since the early 1600s but was much neglected until the nineteenth century. No.47, on the corner, has an old sundial inscribed 'I.C.F', dating from the early or mid-eighteenth century and No.49 Linton Cottage dates from the late seventeenth or early eighteenth century.

If you wish to walk up the steep street, at the upper end note No.105, which is partly eighteenth-century and has a 'Farmers Fire & Life' insurance fire-mark. Nos. 80, 86, and 93 are similar eighteenth-century thatched cottages.

THE OLD READING ROOM, opposite Linton Cottage, was built in 1926 to commemorate those killed in the First World War. There was also a library and a bathhouse, where you could get baths for a tanner (6d.), and it was a surgery for a time. It was a very popular meeting place for the village ladies.

Turn right at the crossroads.

THE OLD BAKEHOUSE, on the right, is eighteenth-century or earlier. It has a large central room with a very large beam, where the ovens and chimney used to be. Note the top window on the roadside, where sacks of flour would have been hoisted in.

THE OLD BAKERY, next door, has a later brick extension at the rear. The bakery went out of business in 1968, apparently because the bread was so disgusting! No doubt it was also because of the competition from outside deliveries.

WHITEHORSE COTTAGE, possibly dating from the late sixteenth century, used to be an inn, which was closed by 1887. It was also a house of ill-repute, a 'most horrible low place' as George Dew described it in 1861. In 1865, he was also commenting that 'The girls of Heyford are very bad. There are few good'! In 1867, a couple who were seen committing adultery in the carriage of a stationary train, were given the 'rough music' treatment outside their homes on three

Freehold Street looking east with Dews' Shop and Post Office on the left , postcard 1920s (David Dare).

consecutive evenings. This was also called 'skimmington' or 'lewbelling' i.e. lewd + belling! This was the normal punishment for cuckolds or wife beating. 'The rattle was most noisy; all the old tin and iron utensils I should think to be found in both parishes were rattling'. His criticism of the village continued in 1875 on the death of Ann Tustin, who he said was 'widely regarded as a witch'.[6]

PURCELL COTTAGE (No.32), on the corner; the village was still called Heyford Purcell in the nineteenth century. Note the telephone kiosk outside, which was designed by Sir Giles Gilbert Scott in 1935.

THE OLD POST OFFICE, next to No.25, used to be a ladies' boarding school kept by the Misses Hore in the nineteenth century. Mary Hore was also publican at The Bell in 1852! The Post Office was here for c.120 years and finally closed in 1995.

FORGE HOUSE (No.17) is probably seventeenth-century, altered in the eighteenth century. The rear wing seems to be a later addition. There is also a thatched stone outbuilding to the rear. There used to be a coal yard next door. John Dew (1809-74), father of George and John, lived here. He was a builder and baker and ran a grocery and ironmongery. John took over from his father and published Dews Almanac in the 1880s, in which he offered 'Xmas cards, note paper, bookbinding, books and picture framing'. He also delivered London newspapers to 14 parishes 'every morning by special messengers'. The Dews also owned another shop across the road.

PAINE'S COTTAGE (No.20), opposite, dates from the late seventeenth or early eighteenth century, with the left half of the front being the oldest part. A photograph c.1910 indicates that there may have been a shop here. The large thatched extension to the left with two garage doors, and 'The Wings' next door, are both twentieth-century. The name may have a connection with Steeple Aston, where Paine's Hill is named after John Paine, butcher, auctioneer, and owner of the Fleur de Luce Inn.

The first WESLEYAN METHODIST CHAPEL used to stand in the garden next to Forge House. It was built in the early nineteenth century by Thomas Rose, the miller. It was an old wooden building with steps up to it, as Nellie Stockford recalled from going to Sunday School there in the early 1900s.

COLLEGE FARM HOUSE, formerly Knapton's Farmhouse, on the corner, is late seventeenth- or early eighteenth-century. It is a three-unit through-passage plan, with upper windows from the eighteenth or early nineteenth century. The barn next door, now called Town House, is early eighteenth-century.

MERRY'S FARMHOUSE, formerly Manor Farm and Glebe Farm, on the corner of The Lane, used to have its farm buildings in the present Knapton's Croft. The 1606 map shows it as L-shaped with the larger part running north-south. The cellar is now filled in. There used to be a door on the street end. This was the home of the Merrys in the sixteenth and seventeenth centuries. They were millers in the village until 1845 when the last Merry emigrated to the United States. Blomfield says 'he has never since been heard of, the common rumour being that he there met with a violent death from the hands of the companion who migrated with him'.[7]

THE MARKET PLACE was the centre of the old village, which stretched from the manors to the mill. The 1606 map shows houses round and in the middle of the square, with the Town House and other houses along the main street to the east. It was still used as a market place in the nineteenth century, and there were cattle and sheep sales until 1889. The Jubilee Oak was planted in 1887 for

The Market Place with The Bell Inn and College Farm, 1920s (OCC).

Queen Victoria's Golden Jubilee (see the plaque), and the stone seat round it commemorates the Millennium.

Note the following in the Market Place:

The BELL INN dates from the late seventeenth and early eighteenth century. It is first mentioned in 1819 but it may have been a pub as early as the sixteenth century. It was originally three houses. Note the old newel staircase projection at the rear. In 1852, the publican, Mary Hore, was also running a ladies boarding school! By 1876, James Collingridge was the publican and he was succeeded by his wife, Mary. In the 1940s, there used to be a fish and chip shop next door in the early eighteenth-century thatched outbuilding.

The butcher's shop used to be opposite, the forge was in the OWL'S NEST, and the dairy in the BUTTERHOUSE.

GLEBE COTTAGE (No.5) is a very well preserved sixteenth-century cottage with original stairs and an old inglenook. It still belongs to Corpus Christi College.

HAYSTON BARN, opposite the Old School, used to be part of Knapton's.

THE OLD SCHOOL used to be the National School but is now a private house. It was built in 1868 for about 100 children, having opened in 1867 in the house next door. There is also a datestone

'AD1894', which must have been the date of an extension.

Typically, George Dew was involved in the opening of the school and it was called the Mary Dew School (see the plaque) after Mary whom he married in 1872. She taught there from 1867 to 1913 and Dorothy Dew, their daughter, taught for 50 years from 1889 to 1939!

In 1808, there were two Dame schools teaching reading, writing, and knitting for 60 children. By 1833, there were two fee-paying schools (one of them for farmers' daughters), and a third one where a Thomas Rose legacy supported four children. They were probably Methodists as it was he who built the first Wesleyan chapel. In 1854, there were still three schools. Nationally there was widespread opposition to schools for much of the nineteenth century because it was thought that they spoiled girls for domestic service, overeducated the poor, and anyway parents needed their children to work.

No.17 with a gable-end, to the right of the school, used to be the old shop (Miss Reason's). The drive past Redbury Cottage (No.15) and Nos.12 and 13 used to lead to Grantham's Wharf.

You can now retrace your steps down Church Lane to the church.

Notes

1   Peter Deeley, *Valley of the Cherwell: Its People and Places* (2001), 50.
2   Pamela Horn (ed.), *The Diaries of George James Dew* (1983 and 1986).
3   Pamela Horn (ed.), *Oxfordshire Village Life: The Diaries of George James Dew (1846-1928).*
5   *Victoria County History of Oxford*, vi (Ploughley Hundred), 193.
6   Pamela Horn (ed.), *The Diaries of George James Dew (1846-1928), Relieving Officer* (1983).
7   J.C. Blomfield, quoted by Peter Deeley, 47.

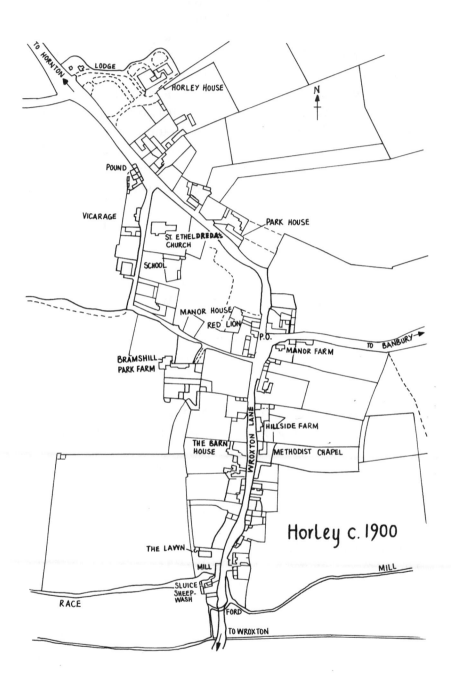

Horley c. 1900

Chapter 5

Horley

The ancient parish of Horley lies in the extreme north-west of Oxfordshire on the Warwickshire boundary, some three miles from the Edgehill escarpment and four miles from Banbury. It can be reached off the A423 Banbury to Southam road. In the Domesday Book, the three villages of Hornton, Horley, and Upton, which has disappeared (apart from Upton House), were all collated under one name, Hornlie, which means 'clearing in a tongue of land'. In 1100, Henry I created a Prebendal Manor of the three manors, granted to the Bishop of Lincoln.

The villages of Horley and Hornton have been connected as far back as time goes. This connection continued with generations of labourers from both villages working in the stone quarries on Edgehill and near Hornton. The first mention of the Hornton quarries was in 1609. The last quarry, Carrs Pit, east of Varney's Garage on the Hornton road, closed in 1942. In the nineteenth century, stone quarrymen could earn £2 a week compared to a possible 13s. for labourers. The Stanley family were masons for generations, with a firm based on Edgehill. Horley and Hornton may have been closely connected over the years but Flora Thompson's aunt wrote of Hornton, where she lived, that 'it was not the place to be after dark.'[1] This was probably because of all the quarrymen out for a drink in the various pubs. About 1865, Bishop Wilberforce even described Hornton as the 'fringe of civilization', though whether he was referring to the geographical position, its morality or the state of the church building is not recorded.[2]

Most of the old houses in Horley were built between c.1580 and 1640 but today very few of them survive. Many of them may have been destroyed during the Civil War. The Banbury to Warwick Road used to run through Horley and Hornton and it would have been much used at that time. Under the Enclosure Act of 1766, the main beneficiaries were Edward Metcalfe of Horley Manor (252 acres), Sir Mordaunt Cope of Bramshill (219 acres), and the Vicar (181 acres). There were 18 farmers then, and the large number of 27 landed proprietors – a clear indication that Horley was an 'open' village. By 1852, there were just 5 farmers and there were the same number in 1939. By 1986, there were just 3, with a similar number in Hornton.

The population of Horley in 1801 was 269 rising to a peak of 425 in 1841. By 1901, it had declined to 247 and in 1991 it was still only 296, although there has been some new building recently. In the early nineteenth century, there were a number of plush-weavers in Horley and Hornton. The industry declined in Banbury from the 1820s and gradually disappeared from the villages in the late nineteenth century. The isolation of Horley and Hornton meant that local craftsmen and small traders persisted longer than elsewhere. The villages were also a good remote location for Puritans and Dissenters. The 1852 trade directory listed 17 trades, including 5 stonemasons. In 1915, there were still 13 trades listed but by 1928 there were only 6. For some forty years from the 1870s, William Coleman was the butcher and John Stamp the shoemaker. In the late nineteenth century, the whole village became an orchard growing Bramley apples, which have great preserving attributes. Many of them were stored in the barn at the back of the Apple Barn House before being taken to Covent Garden or other markets. Today the village has a pub but no school or shop.

Carrier links with Banbury, which started with Hornton in 1811 and with Horley in 1814, generally combined the two villages. Horley's main links were with The Windmill at 56 North Bar, next door to Banbury Parish Church. The Horley carrier operated on Mondays, Thursdays, and Saturdays for most of the period from 1814 until the early 1900s. After that, Jack Sumner from Hornton served both villages with his horse and cart and later with his bus. He was a pioneer in the improvement of public transport, by having his Ford motor adapted by Simmons, coachbuilders in Bridge Street. His 1926 bus had the discomfort of hard wooden seats but held more passengers than his cart and as such was superior to that of most village carriers.[3]

We begin our walk at the top of the hill at St Etheldreda's Church (GR 417439).

ST ETHELDREDA'S CHURCH, judging by its shape and size, is an
    enlargement of a Saxon church. St Etheldreda was a seventh-century
    Anglian Princess who founded Ely Cathedral. The church is notable
    for the huge St Christopher painting on the north aisle wall and for its

St Etheldreda's Church, with Colonel Stockton's farm wagon by the old entrance to the rickyard, 1930s (OCC).

lightness, as there is virtually no stained glass; perhaps it was all destroyed during the Civil War.

12th century: the central tower dates from c.1100, with two belfry windows from c.1200.

13th century: the chancel dates from c.1200, including the aumbry (recess) with the dog-tooth ornament. The tub-shaped font may also be of this date. The church was remodelled in this century and the arcades are remarkably tall and stately for a village church.

14th century: c.1320 the building was enlarged, with the addition of the clerestory and the south porch and an extended south aisle. Both arcades may have been remodelled then. The fine Romanesque pillared doorway was moved to its present position at the west end. Outside, the tower was buttressed and the scratch sundial was made in the south-west corner (repaired in 1993).

15th century: the great St Christopher wall painting, on the north aisle wall, dates from c.1450: 'One of the largest and most perfect representations of this saint in the country'.[4] Note the dogfish which have been given dogs' heads! The poor ate dried dogfish, which came headless, so the fish would have been unknown by sight to the medieval painter. There is also some painting on the south wall and some crude rings with anchors on the wall by the chancel arch. In the north aisle there are two rare pieces of old glass dating from c.1420; they show Henry Rumworth, who became Archdeacon at Canterbury, and his successor in the rectory, Robert Gilbert, later Bishop of London.

19th-20th centuries: some later features of the church include the Gothic Revival pulpit, installed in 1836. By 1915, the whole church was in a ruinous state and the Revd Harold Buxton instituted a general restoration by William Weir. In 1950, thanks to a generous legacy from John Clement Ansell of Horley Manor, further restoration and adornment of the church was carried out by Lawrence Dale, including the striking rood-screen and loft.

Other items of interest include:

a) In the north aisle, an old hand-bier, an old Parish oak chest with three locks dating from 1713 (date on the front plate), and the old Table from the Methodist Chapel dating from 1637.

b) A fine domestic chamber organ near the west door, built in 1765. It was made or repaired by Irvien of London and was re-conditioned in 1965.

c) In the north-west corner, a splendid Victorian coke-burner, surmounted by a crown, made by Gurneys Ventilating Co.

d) Just outside the south porch the slab-top tomb of Michael Harding (d.1627), a notable benefactor of the village who lived next door in the Master's House.

ROWARTH HOUSE, opposite, the former vicarage, was built c.1667. By 1790, it was 'in ruins' and the present building is mainly mid-nineteenth-century. In 1915, the Revd Harold Buxton undertook restoration of the vicarage when the church was being restored. The back of the house is now the front!

Take the path from the south door across the churchyard, noting that the village Green used to run from here to the mill at the bottom of Wroxton Lane.

The OLD NATIONAL SCHOOL and MASTER'S HOUSE are on the site of a thatched cottage dating from c.1580, where Michael Harding, a yeoman, was born. When he died in 1627, he left a house, garden, and land, including fourteen acres in Neithrop, to support the school and master. The Michael Harding Trust survives to this day and still owns the cottage and school buildings.

The Master's House was enlarged in 1771, the date on the chimney-

The Manor House – façade c.1945 (OCC).

stack. In 1842, a Gothic schoolroom was added and you can see the Church of England plaque of that date. In 1860, there were 46 pupils daily. In 1899, a new brick extension was erected, when there were 50 pupils, and there is a datestone on the south end. In the 1960s, a further extension was added. Morag Saunders was a much-loved headteacher for the last thirteen years before the school closed in the 1960s. The children now go to Hornton. The building has reopened as a Field Study Centre for Banbury and other local schools.

Follow the passage, or 'ginnel', towards the Manor House. On the way, note the in-filled garden doorway, which used to give a short cut to the church, and the fine old barn on the right in the Manor orchard.

The MANOR HOUSE has an elegant front dating from c.1700. The long east-west range, which is L-shaped with mullioned windows, dates from the sixteenth and seventeenth centuries. It stands on the site of the earlier prebendal (church) manor house. The lay manor land was bought in 1544 and 1580 by Christopher Light, who sold it

Bramshill Park Farm, with Mrs Astell, Peter Astell and Miss Walden c.1920 (Mary Riley).

to Daniel Danvers in 1617. Danvers is reputed to have lived at Bramshill Park opposite, so perhaps he built the Manor House at this time. In 1624, he sold it to John Austin. In 1718, Nathaniel Austin may have remodelled the eastern façade, when he also acquired Manor Farm on Wroxton Lane.

By 1802, there was no person 'of note' in Horley! But by 1852 the manor was a 'gentleman's residence'. In 1899, William Charles Bagnall was living here. In 1920 he was succeeded by his son, William Cole Bagnall, who afterwards moved to Holly Tree Farm. After them, Colonel Arthur Stockton lived here for many years, while his son, John, lived at Manor Farm. Note the ancient mulberry tree on the corner.

BRAMSHILL PARK FARM was originally the lay manor house, and represents the surviving southern portion of a much larger house. The northern wing was reputedly destroyed by fire, and you may still be able to see some blackened stones on the north wall. The remaining southern part dates from the sixteenth and seventeenth centuries. The Danvers family owned it from 1617 to 1668, when

'When it comes to looks': W.S. Astell's farm wagon in 1936 when he was farming at Bramshill Park Farm, pictured in *Country Fair*, January 1959 (Mary Riley).

Richard Thomson bought it. He lived here until 1718 and the rectangular bay projecting from the east front has the initials T.R.D. (Richard Thomson and his wife) on the head of the lead drain-pipes. In 1718, the property was acquired by Sir John Cope, who had lost the title to Hanwell Castle. He renamed it Bramshill, after family holdings in Hampshire, although he never lived here. He also acquired Park Farm, now Park House, next to the new vicarage.

By the time of the 1766 Enclosure, Sir Mordaunt Cope was the owner. He grew sloe bushes and willows for hurdles for division of the fields. Sloe bushes are still to be seen above the fish-ponds by Horley Brook. In Old Manor Court, below Bramshill, the seventeenth-century outbuildings, including Mulberry Barn and Bramshill Barn, have all been modernised. There is also further development taking place below them.

From 1909, Mary Riley's father, William Astell, was a tenant farmer of Sir Anthony Cope here. After his death, she and her brother, Peter, continued as tenants and after Peter's death, Mary farmed here until 1989. The Rileys bred shire-horses but during the First World War they were left with just four old horses, as the rest were taken to the Front. They also lost all their labourers except for two old men. After the War, they continued to breed and use shire-horses until tractors took over in the 1940s. During the Second World War, they had to rely for labour on German and Italian POWs. The Copes sold the house in 1989.

Walk down Little Lane to the junction with Wroxton Lane, known as The Square, and turn right down the hill.

Wroxton Lane

Note the grass verges which survive from the old Village Green.
Gullivers Close opposite is now a housing estate but there used to be many fine walnut trees here. From the 1890s, 'Holy Joe' John Griffin, who lived at Prospect Cottage on the corner of the Close, was farming here; he was also a horse-dealer and he used to keep landaus in his sheds. He was an active member of the Salvation Army and his name is on their Citadel in George Street, Banbury as one of the founders. He was quarrelsome and never stopped talking. After he died, railings were put round his grave and it was said that 'you needed to jump on his grave to keep him in'!

THE JAYS is on the site of the old New Inn, where a cellar was found during construction. There used to be a forge 'topside' of it.

HILARY COTTAGE, on the right, used to be a small shop run by the Matthews family from the 1870s. Charles, James, Percy, John and later Mrs Matthews all ran the shop.

HILLSIDE FARM opposite was once a main farm, with mullioned windows and an old granary behind. There are fragments of thirteenth-century stonework still visible in the walls. In the nineteenth and twentieth centuries it was in two halves. The north half housed the village's first Post Office and you can see its bricked-up front door. The south end, with a cellar, was a dairy.

CHAPEL COTTAGE below may have been the first house on the Green and it still has a circular bake oven to the rear. It retains an old frontage with drip-stone mullion windows.

WESLEYAN CHAPEL: in 1794 Barnes Bourton Hirons gave his walnut orchard to the village Methodists so that they could build a chapel. By 1800, the chapel had been completed and it was the first Methodist chapel to be built outside Banbury. The 1851 religious census records that 75 attended service here in the morning and 90 in the evening. There were still many shag-weavers in the village then, and most of them were staunch Methodists. The chapel has been converted to a private dwelling and the Warmington Chapel (1811) is now the oldest one on the Banbury Circuit still in use. The following notes show the past strength of Nonconformity in the village.

Nonconformists [5]

a) Prior to the building of chapels, many 'Conventicles' i.e. illegal meetings of Nonconformists, were held in the Banbury area. One in Horley in 1693 was led by Nathaniel Kinch of Horley, who was licensed to teach at any meeting in the county. It was attended by over 100 people, including gentlemen!

b) In 1656, Horley was in the lists of the Midland Association of General Baptists. In 1733, the village was a member of the General Assembly of General Baptists, when it was the only such community in Oxfordshire. They believed in the individual's responsibility to work for his soul's salvation, while other Baptists believed in predestination. In 1768, the christening of two adult Anabaptists was recorded. This sect promoted adult baptism, shared property, and did not allow any secular interference.

c) In 1790, Elizabeth Adams's house and one other house were licensed for services in Horley. Her house may have been used by the Quakers, who were well supported in Banburyshire. The 1851 census records that 40 Primitive Methodists attended evening service in Horley and an average of 60 in the morning. They did not have a chapel and this meeting may have begun as the group which in 1831 was meeting in the house of William Salmons.

The APPLE BARN HOUSE, formerly The Barn House and The Firs, has a nineteenth-century façade of Hornton stone. Most of the building is much older and the old line of the thatch is still visible. Numerous houses in the area had a similar face-lift in the nineteenth century, which makes dating them very difficult. This was a substantial property and used to include the site of Mulberry Barn, the new house behind it. The block to the right used to be for wood, the traps, and stables.

In the late nineteenth century, many of the local Bramley apples were stored in the barn at the back until they were taken to Covent Garden or other markets. The loading bays for the horses and carts used to be at the adjoining Rose Acre (formerly Rose Cottage). Each county had a different colour for its carts and the Oxfordshire ones were yellow. William Coleman lived at Rose Cottage for over forty years and had his butcher's shop at the back.

THE JASMINES, opposite Rose Acre, was once a row of small seventeenth-century cottages for labourers. In the 1920s and 1930s, William Hick lived here and he and his wife used to act as foster-parents. William worked at Bramshill and he was also the local pig-sticker, while his wife took in laundry. John Russell, who also worked at Bramshill, was one of their foster-children.

The 'Happy Hour Meeting Room' used to adjoin The Jasmines. The roof-line of the old Meeting Room seems to show on the wall and an outside wall survives. It was set up as a Temperance Room, probably in the 1890s, and 'Holy Joe' Griffin ran the meetings.

MIDHILL and IVY COTTAGE are twin-gabled buildings with infill between. In 1794, Samuel Endall, a wealthy farmer, built a row of cottages on the site of Midhill called Shagweavers' Cottages; they faced north to avoid sunlight on the cloth. In 1797, Richard Gardiner bought these cottages for his two sons, Thomas, a staunch Methodist, and John, who were both shag-weavers. By the 1820s, weaving was on the decline in Banbury and both brothers turned to stone masonry. John moved to Hornton, as did many local weavers, to work in the quarries there. Thomas Gardner (sic) eventually sold his cottage to Timothy Cobb, a Mayor of Banbury.

The MIDHILL TENEMENTS were built c.1900. Two blocks lay to the south of Midhill and two across the road on the site of the garden and garages of Rivendell. Most of the tenements have been pulled down or turned into garages. In 1900, there were 90 people living in the Tenements.

RIVENDELL used to be two-up, two-down, with a central passage, and it still retains its low central interior beams. Major modernisation was undertaken in 1997, including an extension on the north end.

PHLOX COTTAGE and THE WISHING WELL, on the left, both have low beams and inglenook fireplaces. The Wishing Well used to be a shop and has an annexe at the lower end which used to be a cottage called the Nut Hatch. Note the old gable-end with the former thatch line and a door filled in on the front. In the eighteenth century, there was a small flower-garden on the frontage, as there were at The Jasmines and Marine Cottage.

GREYSTONES, opposite, with the gable-end to the street, was origi-nally two cottages, evidenced by the different style of chimneys. From 1919 the house became part of The Lawn Orphanage and the orphan girls were housed here. In the grounds there is an example of an early fifteenth- or sixteenth-century one-up, one-down cottage, partially altered in the nineteenth century. Originally, it had small windows unglazed but with wooden bars. Upstairs there was just a

The Wroxton Lane ford with the old Mill and Mill House on the left in 1914 (OCC).

storeroom for wool, cheese, bacon, and apples. It has now been
totally modernised.

THE LAWNS, on the right, became The Poor Law Children's Home of
North Oxfordshire c.1915, when it was run by Mr and Mrs Walter
Wedd. Oliver Stockton had lived here prior to the opening of the
Home. In 1939, Mr and Mrs C.G. Carter were listed as foster-parents
here. In 1950, it was still listed as a Children's Home with Mrs
Wakeman as the matron. The east end of the house appears to be a
nineteenth-century addition, while the rest dates from the eighteenth
century or earlier. The children were allowed to use the bottom of the
close belonging to Bramshill as a playground. In exchange the Home
sent two strong boys to help the Rileys at harvest time. The Home
closed in the 1950s and the house was sold.

HORLEY MILL: the garage on the right with a circular window, just
before the house called Horley Mill, was the site of the eighteenth-
century water corn mill. There was a mill recorded in Horley at
Domesday and a miller worked here until 1924. Between the Wars,
children were taken to the Mill House to be weighed on the mill's
large weighing-machine. If you walk along the brook to the right, you
will see the medieval mill race and two fish-ponds put there by Sir

John Cope of Bramshill Park in the eighteenth century.

The IRONSTONE WORKS, which began to operate early in the 1900s between Hornton and the A422 Stratford road, ran the mill for food for their horses. The tracks for the steam train, which carried the ironstone to Banbury, were laid by German POWs during the First World War. The tracks ran just below the New Inn at Wroxton Heath. The last train ran in 1968. The prisoners also built the bridge over Wroxton Brook in 1916 and it is still called the German Bridge. During the Second World War, some of the Italian prisoners were very angry when they discovered that many of their number were 'making iron-ore to bomb Italy'.

BROOK COTTAGE, on Wroxton Brook, has been totally modernised. In 1784, the brook was diverted to serve a new mill in Horley and the old Moor Mill in Hanwell Parish. This caused some distress by flooding the road from Horley to Wroxton. There used to be a ford here.

Retrace your steps to The Square.

MANOR FARM HOUSE, the three-storey gabled building on the right, dates from the seventeenth and eighteenth centuries. In 1718, Nathaniel Austin from The Manor acquired it. More recently, John Stockton, son of the Colonel, lived here. Note the blocked windows, the later extension on the roadside, and the old barn on the left.

There used to be an old cottage on the corner opposite where Colonel Stockton's cook lived. There was also a small shop next to it.

Along Banbury Lane, STONEBORO COTTAGE and MULBERRY COTTAGE, formerly Thorn Cottage, have both been modernised.

The CRICKET GROUND lies beyond them. There was cricket in the village in the inter-war years, when it was played in a meadow by The Brook, but no formal records survive. In 1941, the Revd Morgan, who was a great enthusiast, formed a club and they played on a flat field behind the Old Vicarage. This was with the enthusiastic agreement of Bob Hamer who lived at Horley House. The Club was formally started on the present site in 1948 and celebrated its fiftieth anniversary in 1998.

LION COTTAGE opposite Manor Farm: note the old thatch line, the other old cottages below, and the old mullion window in The Cottage. After Enclosure in 1766, affluent farmers split their houses

The Square with the New Inn, the Red Lion, and old cottages c.1907-10 (OCC).

and built adjoining cottages to accommodate poor labourers and dispossessed farmers. Mrs Rump ran the Post Office and a little shop in the cottage below Lion Cottage for over thirty years. She came from Norfolk with her husband in the 1930s, when he was employed as a stockman by Colonel Stockton.

The RED LION: in the nineteenth century there were five licensed houses in the village, including The Crown (1783), The Buck (1786), and The Bull (1806). Later there was also the New Inn opposite and there are mentions of The Star and The Gooseberry Bush. There used to be a bakehouse behind the Red Lion run by Mr Prickett. There are hollow ways in Horley and Hornton. These were sunken lanes, which may have been Saxon estate boundaries. The hollow way here runs up the hill above the inn, passing the churchyard on the left.

PARK HOUSE, formerly Park Farm, up the hill on the right next to the new vicarage, is partly medieval. There was an original three-unit plan with two ground floor rooms on different levels, separated by a through-passage. At the rear, you can still see an Early English style doorway, with a possible set of Romanesque pillars, a three-light mullion window and a blocked thirteenth-century decorated slit window. This may have lit a family chapel room. There is also an old

well and an old barn, now the garage of the new house next door. In
1718, Sir John Cope bought the house when he acquired Bramshill.
There is a legend that there were monks in Horley, who may have
been Monks of St Peter at Park House. They would have left in the
fourteenth century during the Hundred Years War. The house was
modernised in 1987.

HOLLY TREE FARM and DAIRY COURT, on the hill above Park
House: in 1903 William Cole Bagnall was farming here before he
took over from his father at the Manor House c.1920. Later he
returned to Holly Tree Farm.

ESSEX HOUSE, at the top of the hill, probably dates from the eighteenth century, with a later rear extension.

Opposite, there used to be a large POUND where stray animals were
confined and a fine was paid to retrieve them. It used to stretch from
POUND COTTAGES, next to Rowarth House, to the watering pond
which lies under the front garden of the last house on the west of the
Hornton Road. Note the row of old cottages including Church
Cottage, The Old Smithy, and Wood Cottage.

MELLING COTTAGE, opposite on the corner of Horley Gardens,
seems to be a survivor from a row of terraced houses which was built
here c.1795. It has an original small square window on the roadside.
If you walk down Horley Gardens towards Bayliss Orchard, note the
old barn on the left which belongs to Horley Cottage.

HORLEY COTTAGE, the long L-shaped building next to Melling
Cottage, was a farm from the seventeenth or eighteenth century.

HORLEY HOUSE: between c.1725 and 1750 the Austin family altered
the house considerably, re-modelling it and giving it a Georgian front.
It was enlarged c.1851 by John Hitchcock, one of the principal
landed proprietors, who was living here by 1852. There are some fine
trees and a walled garden from this period. In those days there was an
old road direct from the Warwick road to the rear of the house. There
used to be a line of cottages on the roadside, which appears to have
been demolished in the late nineteenth century.

After Hitchcock, a series of military men occupied the house, including
Major Maul who played cricket for Warwickshire and England and
was Mayor of Banbury. He was living here by 1899 and kept six
servants. There is a memorial in the church to one of his sons who
was killed in the Great War. The house used to supply water to the
village from some dozen large tanks in the roof. The house has been

reduced in size. During the Second World War, German POWs lodged here, with barbed wire round the walls and sentries posted. After the War, Alcan bought the property but unfortunately their records have been destroyed.

HORLEY LODGE, with its iron gates, appears to be a classic Victorian lodge and was probably built by John Hitchcock when he was enlarging Horley House in the 1850s.

You can now retrace your steps to the church.

Notes

1   J.P. Bowes, *Walking Through the Centuries* (1991), 67;

2   *Victoria County History of Oxford*, ix (Bloxham Hundred), 125.

3   Brian Little, *Banbury – A History*, 85.

4   Sherwood & Pevsner, *The Buildings of England: Oxfordshire* (1974), 653.

5   *Victoria County History of Oxford*, ix (Bloxham Hundred), 137.

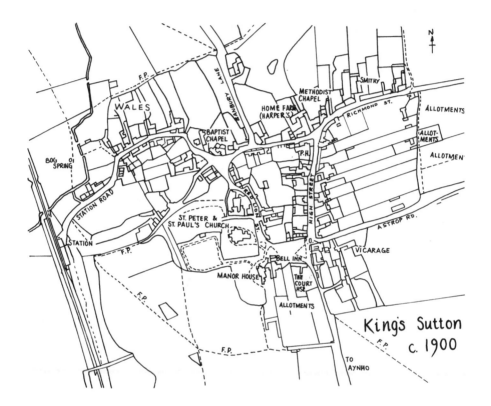

Kings Sutton
c. 1900

Chapter 6

King's Sutton

King's Sutton is about a mile off the B4100 Aynho to Adderbury road and only five miles from Banbury. It is the only selected village not in Oxfordshire, but it has an Oxfordshire postcode and is clearly within Banburyshire. It is one of the largest parishes in England, covering some thirty square miles. There is evidence of a Roman settlement and the Portway runs close by from Aynho to Walton Grounds. The village was part of the Royal Estates from Saxon times when Alfred bequeathed it to his kinsman, Osric. It was called 'Suttun Regis' then and this name survived until the seventeenth century. In the Domesday Book it is listed as 'Svdtone', which means South Farm, and there was a market here, worth 20s. a year to the King. The name 'Kinges Sutton' is first mentioned in 1294.

The discovery of a medicinal spring at nearby Astrop after the Civil War heralded the start of an era of prosperity for Astrop and King's Sutton. The spring was discovered in April 1664 by Drs Lower and Willis. Dr Radcliffe, the famous Oxford physician, regularly patronised it. Celia Fiennes, on her travels round England, commented c.1694 that 'I went to Astrop where is a Steele water much frequented by ye Gentry, it has some mixture of Allom so is not so strong as Tunbridge.'[1] In 1740, Dr Thomas Short suggested that it was a cure for seventy conditions. At the height of its fame, there was a public ball every Monday, with cards, dancing, and a variety of social events. The Revd John Russell Greenhill, rector of Fringford (1756-1813), mentions in his diaries going to the Astrop Ball and Supper in the 1780s.

But fashion changed. By 1777, Astrop was out of fashion and Leamington Spa had become 'the place' to take the waters, although Thomas Rowlandson did paint the Spa at Astrop in 1813. After the first decade of the nineteenth century, as new spas such as Leamington opened, a great silence, one writer noted, fell upon King's Sutton. By 1914, you could just about make out the ruins of the tearoom and the assembly hall. The original well is now in very poor condition. In 1749, a new well, the Bog Spring, was opened in a meadow by King's Sutton station. In 1900, Edwin Walford mentioned 'the other mineral spring charged with sulphate of soda, yet in common use by the people of the homesteads.'[2]

The village was enclosed in 1804, with the main beneficiaries being William Shippen Willes (660 acres), George and William Lovell (146 acres), and Edward Jenkinson (112 acres). 228 acres were shared between 32 landowners and 52 owners of cottages and gardens, making King's Sutton another example of an 'open' village. In 1801, the population was 1,021, rising to a peak of 1,335 in 1851, when there were 14 farmers and 61 traders. This prosperity was partly due to the increased use of the nearby Oxford Canal. By 1901, the population had declined to 1,101 and by 1906 there were only 4 farmers and 42 trades listed in the trade directory. By 1940, there were only 27 trades. By 1961, the population had risen to 1,550 and by 1991 to 2,082. This was largely due to the new housing built up the Astrop and Richmond Roads, starting in the 1960s.

Carrier links with Banbury began as early as 1796, with journeys by Richard Owen to The White Lion three times a week. He operated until the late 1820s. There were links with seven inns during the nineteenth century, the longest with the Fleur de Lys in Broad Street (c.1826-84) and the Old George in Cow Fair (c.1853-1906). William Barber was the carrier from c.1864 to 1906, going to the Old George or The Fox, next to the Gaol in the Market Place. He was succeeded by his son, William Edward, who continued until 1939. Pauline Barber still lives in Ivy Cottage, Astrop, where the Barbers have lived since the early 1800s. The carriers' journeys often linked Astrop, Newbottle, Charlton, Overthorpe and Warkworth. Apart from taking produce for sale to market and filling people's shopping lists, the carriers used to take a few passengers, which was a great treat for the younger people. In terms of family continuity, mention should also be made of Percy Ayriss, who was a baker for over fifty years, David Cadd, who was a saddle and harness maker from c.1906 to 1940, and the Cousins family, who were shopkeepers for about a century.

Village Fires and Fire-marks

The village has experienced an unusual number of serious fires. In the Great Fire of 13 July 1785, 40 houses were burnt down, including most of the older houses in Whittall Street, Astrop Road, and The Square. It caused damage amounting to £3,287 16s. 5d.. Some carved stones dating the Great Fire can still be found on various buildings e.g. Holland House in Astrop Road and above the front door of the White Horse. In 1915, a fire destroyed the buildings on Blake's Corner. In 1923, the cottage next to Lovells was burned down during Morning Service. On 29 October 1929, the 'Paradise Fire' destroyed six or seven houses up Paradise Lane, off Red Lion Square. The man who started it by throwing a firework into the thatch was still living until recently! Finally, in 1944, a fire at the bottom of Red Lion Street destroyed the Cousins's shop, the cottage across the road, and the thatch on some of the neighbouring cottages.

It is hardly surprising that several cottages and houses bear the fire-marks of the companies with whom the inhabitants insured. These fire-marks were proof of insurance to the Fire Brigade and also good company advertising. Early ones were lead and often had a policy number on them, while later ones were copper or iron. The earliest fire-engines were provided by Hand in Hand (1707), Sun Fire Office (1716), and Westminster Fire Office (1720).

The Legend of St Rumbald

Legend has it that St Rumbald was born at Walton Grounds a mile from King's Sutton in AD662, son of Rumbald, King of Northumberland and a Saxon princess, but was said to have lived for only three days. He spoke holy words and after professing himself a Christian, was baptised! It seems more likely that the three days refer to his life after baptism. He was buried at Sutton but translated to Brackley and thence to Buckingham, where a shrine was erected for him in the church. In 1537, Leland recorded that 'There was of late a Chapell dedicated to him standing about a mile from Sutton'. This stood in what was called the Chapel Field near the main farmhouse at Walton Grounds. Remnants of old foundations have been found on this site. The Saxon font just inside the church door is associated with the baptism of St Rumbald. It was restored in 1923 after it was re-discovered in the churchyard by the vicar, the Revd William Rennie. He had it placed it on a circular stone from Twyford Mill.

We begin our walk at the church of St Peter and St Paul by The Square (GR 497362).

The CHURCH OF ST PETER and ST PAUL was once the Mother
Church for a large area. The building was started in 1082 on the site

The Square with the spire of St Peter & St Paul's Church, postcard c.1910. The 3-storey cottage next to Lovells was burned down in 1923 (Nick Nice).

of an earlier Saxon church. The living, formerly in the patronage of the Willes family, is now in the gift of The Society for the Preservation of the Faith (a High Anglican/Anglo-Catholic society). The Roman Catholics also hold services in the parish church. The church is currently undergoing substantial repairs.

The magnificent fifteenth-century spire, built between 1400 and 1450, rises to 198 feet, 100 feet above the flying buttresses. Its walls are said to be no thicker than nine inches and it sways both in the wind and when the eight bells are rung. It is one of three great local spires, which can be seen together from certain vantage points and prompted the following saying: 'Adderbury for strength, Bloxham for length, and King's Sutton for beauty'.

Norman: the chancel inside is mainly Norman. On the south side, note the elaborate piscina (for washing hands and vessels). On the north side, there is an ancient aumbry (a small cupboard or recess), with a Victorian door, which would have been used to house the plate and silver. The arcade of pillars on the south side of the Choir is Norman. The south aisle was built c.1220.

14th century: the north aisle was built c.1320 but the north porch was much restored in 1834. The south porch was built c.1350. Note the 'ball flower' ornament over the door. The stoup for holy water sitting in the porch was found by the vicar in a farmyard in Mill Lane in 1922.

16th century: the great west porch with its beautiful vaulted roof was built c.1450. In the Middle Ages, services of baptism and marriage were begun in the porch, and parish business might also be transacted there. On the wall of the porch is an old beam dating from 1686, inscribed with the names of the churchwardens, George Tomes and Michael Covedale, and 'Thomas Williams Fecit' i.e. Thomas Williams made it.

17th century: at the west end of the south aisle you can see the works of the original turret clock, which was installed for £10 in 1696. It had no face but in 1902 it was renovated and given a dial. In 1950, it was finally replaced by a new clock. Outside, there is an ancient stone sundial, possibly of this period, on the parapet above the east end of the south aisle.

19th century: in 1866 the chancel was restored and a new oak screen, designed by Sir Giles Gilbert Scott, at the sole expense of Mrs Willes, replaced the stone screen. The east window commemorates four members of the Willes family. The fine organ by Walker also dates from this time. Note the old stairs to the rood loft, where the Gospel used to be read on Sundays. The west gallery was removed from the tower arch in 1840, and part of it was used for the north porch of Lovells, just across the road. The church was re-seated in 1842.

The Square

The MANOR HOUSE, on the right, was held by the Crown from 1086 to 1156, when Henry II granted it to Richard Camvill. At the time of the Civil War, Richard Kenwrick was the Lord of the Manor. King's Sutton was a Royalist garrison and Kenwrick is reputed to have hidden Charles I in the Manor, which was occupied by soldiers. Cromwell's horse may also have been quartered here at some point.

The present manor house dates from 1650 but contains later additions. It is said to have had a priest's room and an underground escape route to the church (never found).

In 1735, Sir John Willes, who had served as Lord Chief Justice and Attorney General, purchased it but never lived here. The Willes family from Warwickshire also built Astrop House. The manor was deserted from 1735 until 1826, when William Willes succeeded to the estate and married Sophia Cartwright from Aynho. He died in 1865 but Sophia lived here until her death in 1896. The Manor was then sold to Lewis Selby-Bigge. Later Colonel and Mrs Fisher lived here; she was a Miss Brown from Astrop House.

The CRICKET CLUB was founded in 1861 but records survive only from 1922, when the Club was playing on a ground at the rear of the Manor House. In 1924, they made their headquarters at The Bell Inn next door. In 1946, they moved to Astrop Park and in 1968 to their present site on the Charlton Road. Since then they have had considerable success in a number of competitions.

BELL HOUSE was the Bell Inn until the early 1990s. The east end dates from 1620 but there were many alterations c.1720. The stable wing behind has some picturesque arched windows, similar to those of 4 Red Lion Street. Outside, note the remains of the stocks which were last used in 1858.

The COURT HOUSE is a building of rich architectural character dating from c.1500. It was extended later in the sixteenth century, and again in the eighteenth century, when a further extension was built on the south end. Apart from Q Cottage on Station Road, it is the only surviving building in the region outside Banbury itself which has fragments of timber-framed walling, probably dating from the sixteenth century. Both have stone walls to the ground floor with timber studding above, jettied over the stonework. Originally, it was a basic three-room house of cross-passage plan, with a very wide entrance passage and broad stairs. It was probably used both as the Manorial Court House and as a dwelling. The Court Room survives on the east end.

Such quality of the detail and craftsmanship in carpentry and joinery is rarely found in the region outside Banbury. Note, for example, the entrance door and the wood moulding on the north front. Inside, there are some fine fireplaces and timberwork, with a staircase dating from the late sixteenth century in the projection at the east end.[3]

The WHITE HORSE was thatched until recent times and bears a plaque above the porch recording 'A Great Fire on July 13 1785' (now barely legible).

The Co-op, later Coupe's Grocery Store, used to be on the corner of Astrop Road next to the pub. There was also a butcher's shop here.

The MONKS' COTTAGES, on the north side of The Square, date from the seventeenth century but were altered in the nineteenth and twentieth centuries. They are reputed to have been used as lodgings for the monks or priests when the parish church was the Mother Church. Apart from Corner Cottage, the cottages are still thatched and some mullion windows survive. The cottage nearest to Lovells has a very fine old well. There used to be another picturesque three-storey cottage in the walled garden of Lovells but it was burned down during Morning Service in 1923.

LOVELLS is named after the fourteenth-century Lords of the Manor. The house is mainly eighteenth-century but probably dates back to the sixteenth or seventeenth century. It was originally three-room width, with a screens passage leading from the old front door (now closed) on the Square side. The kitchen used to be in the room to the east of the passage. On the north side, there is an open porch, once part of the ringers' gallery, which was moved from beneath the church tower in 1842. This may have been when the rear portion of the building and a room on the east end were added. In the early twentieth century, the front was rendered, giving it a late Georgian appearance but the stonework was exposed again c.1938. Note the tiny windows on the top floor which probably date from the removal of the thatch roof.

Red Lion Street

Most of the cottages on the street were built by tradesmen between the seventeenth and nineteenth centuries and some were thatched until the 1950s. There used to be three shops here. Until mains water came in 1954, eleven households shared a single well at the rear of No.10. At one time there were as many as twenty-six Mr Wyatts living in the village. Most of them lived on Red Lion Street, which caused major confusion for Bert and Gwen Taylor at the Post Office!

The COACH HOUSE, on the corner, used to be part of Lovells. The old entrance for carts was where the stone arch and window now are. It must have been a very steep turn.

No.1 dates from the eighteenth century and was formerly a saddler's shop. The shop-window can still be seen at the lower end, where there is now a garage with a child's wheelbarrow in the window. The building was altered in the nineteenth century.

COBWEB COTTAGE (No.2) has an Eagle Insurance fire-mark, almost hidden by roses. There is a similar fire-mark at No.14.

CHURCH VIEW (No.4) dates from the late eighteenth century and was

Two unusual ledges on the west wall of The Nutshell. The larger one may have been a 'witch-shelf' to provide a perch for passing witches and prevent them entering the house. The smaller one may have been for the witch's cat! (the author).

two dwellings until recently. Note the picturesque arched windows of the period, like those in the stable wing of Bell House. There are three eighteenth-century leaded windows at the first floor on the west side.

COBBLERS (No.11): building started at the 'Bottom End' of the street and at one time this was the last cottage. You can still see where the cobbler had his display-window on the south wall.

Retrace your steps up the street and turn right into Church Avenue.

Church Avenue

SUTTON HOUSE (No.1) is early nineteenth century but it was altered and gentrified in the following century, with sash windows and a panelled central door.

No.2 is a three-storey old stone house with the front door blocked up. It used to be a sweet shop. At the back there is a stone and brick extension, along with an old brewhouse.

The NUTSHELL (No.3), formerly The Walnut Tree Tavern, dates from the sixteenth century and it was thatched until recently. The beams and trusses date it back to c.1550. It was said to have been the meeting place of the carpenters and joiners who worked in the furniture business. Until recently there were still flagstones on the floor and you could see how they had sunk by the old bar where the drinkers used to stand.

Round the corner, there are two unusual ledges on the wall. Local legend has it that the larger one may have been a 'witch-shelf'. The purpose of such a 'shelf' would have been to provide a perch for passing witches and prevent them entering the house. The smaller 'shelf' may have been for the witch's cat! In the sixteenth and seventeenth centuries, there was still a widespread fear of black magic and many bizarre anti-witchcraft devices were used. People thought that witches would bring disease and other misfortune to them and their animals. Such customs go back to remote antiquity and are a remarkable relic of superstition.[4] Given the age of the house, it is quite possible that these ledges were 'witch-shelves'.

The VICARAGE, on the corner, was built in the 1980s to replace the Victorian one in Astrop Road. It is possibly on the site of a medieval one demolished in the nineteenth century. There may also have been another inn here at one time.

LITTLE HILL COTTAGE (No.4) is an old thatched cottage, where one of the trusses dates from 1650. It was once two cottages and there is a blocked door on the north end. The deeds date from 1831 and the property was 'modernised' in this period. Note that the thatch, in common with that on other buildings around The Square, does not have a crest. This seems to be a different style to that used in other local villages.

The Cousins's shop was below here, until it was burned down in the 1944 Fire. Mrs Catherine Cousins was the grocer here before 1900, succeeded sometime before 1914 by John and his wife Annie. Annie moved the shop to No.17 Red Lion Street after the Fire.

Red Lion Square

No.17 Red Lion Street was the home of George Blake before he moved to Blake's Corner. Earlier, it may have been the site of the Red Lion Inn, which dated from c.1700. There are large cellars under the building suitable for storing beer. After the 1944 Fire, it became the home and shop of Annie Cousins, followed by her daughter, Janet, who married George Bevis. The shop finally closed when they retired in 1991. It is a three-storey building, with a two-storey brickwork addition on the north side. This was a separate dwelling where Mrs Hurst ran a small shop. There was another small shop round the corner in an old cottage which has now gone. The whole dwelling has been unoccupied since 1991 and is now in very poor condition.

Red Lion Street, Bottom End: the Cousins's shop was in the house in the centre, which was burned down in the 1944 Fire, postcard c.1910 (Nick Nice).

The OLD BAKERY, opposite the SPINNEY BANK STORES, still has its old 'Hovis Brown' sign, although it closed in the 1990s. Note the tall chimney of the former bakehouse. It was built in 1802 and had a succession of long-serving bakers. Thomas Hopkins was baker for about fifty years before the Great War. Percy Ayriss succeeded his father in 1914 and was the baker for the next fifty years. He used to make deliveries by pony and cart to Aynho, Clifton and later to Souldern Farm. During the Second World War he delivered to the NAAFI, for the troops based at Aynho Park. On Sundays, from 10.30 to 12.30, he cooked joints with Yorkshire pudding and tins of potatoes. The price went up after the Great War to a penny-halfpenny. There was another bakery on Whittall Street. The brick spring outside used to supply the Spinney Bank area. In 1929, the 'Paradise Fire' destroyed six or seven houses up Paradise Lane beyond the Old Bakery.

The BAPTIST CHAPEL, next to the Stores, was built in 1866 (the date-stone is now barely legible). The stone porch was added recently, and a Baptist Church Hall has been built behind. The chapel is typical of the dignified and restrained slightly Gothic Nonconformist buildings of the period. From 1781, local Baptists used to meet in people's

Q Cottage and other old cottages in Station Road, 1930s (Gwen Taylor).

houses and from 1820 in a barn on this site. The 1851 religious
census recorded attendance of 80 in the morning and 116 in the
evening. Baptisms, with total immersion, used to take place in the
nearby River Cherwell, close to Twyford Mill.
The BAPTIST MANSE next door has an elaborate datestone 'Baptist
Manse 1892' confirming its date of construction.
There used to be a timber yard behind the Chapel and the old saw-pits
survive. There are also some allotments and a playing-field here. A
wheelwright/cooper used to live nearby, using the area of the saw-
pits and a large bonfire for working his metal.

Wales Street, formerly Station Road.
Wales Street is perhaps so-called because many men came from Wales
to build the railway and the station in the nineteenth century. It might
also be a corruption of 'wells', of which there are many, including
the Bog Spring. A number of old cottages on the street have vanished
since the 1950s, including an old row from Q Cottage to Studleigh
Farm House. White Cottage (No.5) is an old survivor. No.9, a brick
cottage, may once have been two cottages. No.14, on the right, was
once divided, and you can see where the two front doors used to be.
Q COTTAGE, with the Court House, is one of only two surviving
buildings in the region outside Banbury itself, which have fragments

George Turvey with his milk van on Station Road, 1930s (Gwen Taylor).

of timber-framed walling, probably dating from the sixteenth century. Here the east wall is jettied out at first floor level over the stone ground-floor wall.[5] On the inside, there are indications that the property was once three small cottages.

The unusual name seems to have a naval connection with Q-ships, which were mystery ships disguising their real identity. If so, the name was probably given to the cottage after the First World War. Some may also recall that Q was the Secret Service codename of the 'gadgets-man' in the James Bond books! Some of the old beams in the house may have come from a ship. Note the amazing chimney, which seems to belong in an old fairy tale.

AVONCROFT MEWS is a very recent development on the site of the old garage.

STUDLEIGH FARM HOUSE: there was once a small farm here. The house has been much altered and you can see the differing types of stonework.

RAFTERS (No.19), on the left, was once a small farm with extensive outbuildings. It is a very interesting property, which has been very well researched and restored by the present owners. The deeds go back to 1794 but some fine old beams inside seem to indicate a sixteenth- or seventeenth-century building. The separate cottage at the east end was the original two-storey building, as you can see from the east end wall where the re-pointing by a previous owner is very unfortunate! The old through-passage between the cottage and the barn, which has now been filled in, was the original entrance to the cottage.

The steep pitch of the tiled roof shows that the barn was originally thatched. There used to be a separate outhouse at the west end and there was a roof from the barn to the surviving brick wall until the 1940s. Note the 1898 datestone high on the barn's west wall; this may have been the date when the roof was raised. The fine stone arches over the windows on the street side and at the west end are of interest, as is the rounded corner by the yard entrance – this would have made it easier for the carts. Note also the fine old shutters inside the windows and the changes to the west gable end, where the opening for hay etc has been filled in. In the garden there is a restored privy dating from c.1800. The old pigsties have now been dismantled and re-modelled. There is the site of an old lathe saw in the corner of the yard.

POST CORNER (No.24), with an old GR post box, was probably built in the seventeenth century but is now almost completely late Georgian, with an early Victorian front. The doorway, with support posts to the porch, is worthy of note. There was once a hotel here.

BROOKFIELD HOUSE (No.26) has its drive at the side of Post Corner but the best view of the house is from the field by the Bog Spring. The house dates from the late eighteenth to early nineteenth century. The two-storey section on the north side is said once to have been the brewhouse and kitchen in the seventeenth century (not visible from the road). The Master Tanner lived here c.1850.

DIAMOND JUBILEE COTTAGES (No.23), beyond Rafters, was once a pair of Victorian cottages dated 1897 but is now a single dwelling. The Fire Station used to be beyond them up on the left.

Nos. 42-50, on the right, are a row of mostly nineteenth-century cottages, with some nice early nineteenth-century brickwork. In most cases two cottages have now been combined into one and extended on the back.

Take the path by Willow Cottage (No.50) to the Bog Spring.

The BOG SPRING in Meadow Close was built in 1749. The local inhabitants used to queue here on Sundays, while some drank a daily glass for their health. In 1900, the spring was 'yet in common use by the people of the homesteads.'[6] and it still is. Note the fine view of Brookfield House.

The STATION, at the end of Wales Street: the King's Sutton line was built in 1852 and the station in 1872, in anticipation of the new branch line to Kingham and Cheltenham which opened in 1887. There was extra traffic during the Great War, which led to a longer platform, a footbridge, a waiting room, a ticket office, and engineers' sheds by 1922.

The goods yard had a cattle dock and coal sidings, and there were sidings at nearby Sydenham for the Ironstone Works. The ironstone mines at Sydenham had been worked initially by a cable-car system to the back of the station, and later by a narrow gauge tramway to the sidings just south of the station. Finally the sidings were built at Sydenham itself. The Works were flourishing from the 1870s but closed in 1922, which led to a period of great hardship in the village, with two-thirds of the men out of work. Most of the station buildings were taken down in the 1970s and King's Sutton is now one of only two village stations in Northamptonshire.

Return to Red Lion Square and turn left into Bull's Lane.

Bull's Lane

SUNNY VIEW, next to the Stores, is a small 1897 Victorian villa, with an attractive porch. There used to be a line of old cottages from here to the corner.

The CORNER HOUSE (No.2), at the junction with Banbury Lane, has a datestone 'G.T.1839'. This is probably the date of renovations, since there is evidence of three separate dwellings here before then, with the main and largest one to the left.

No.18, on the right, has a barely legible 1629(?) datestone. The deeds date from 1831 when there were two cottages which were 'modernised' in the 1830s. The little cottage was built on later. The old wooden floor survives with lowered doors, along with an old fireplace and corner stairs.

OLD JOHN'S COTTAGE (No.20): John 'Shoemaker' Wyatt lived here in the late nineteenth and early twentieth centuries. He took part in the Relief of Khartoum in 1884 at the age of 20 and served in the army for 40 years. The cottage has an insurance fire-mark (possibly Eagle) and a datestone '1838 E.F.' Was E.F. related to Robert Fathers at the Bell, who was a builder in 1851?

BLAKE'S CORNER (now a car park) is where George Blake, the

Blake's Corner, before it was demolished in the 1916 Fire, across from Harpers Farm, postcard c.1910 (Nick Nice).

butcher, had his shop. He was a great benefactor of both the Baptist and Methodist churches, and he became a Methodist trustee in 1879. After the fire at his shop on 16 March 1915, a new Methodist Church was to be built on the site. However, it was decided that it would be too dangerous for the children and unsuitable as it was next door to The Three Tuns! For many years the site was left as rubble and called "The Ruins".

Turn right up Whittall Street.

Whittall Street, formerly High Street.
Most of the dwellings on the street date from the seventeenth and eigh-teenth centuries and originally would have been thatched. Many of them must have been damaged in the 1785 Fire and there are numerous signs of alterations in the nineteenth and twentieth centuries. Long closes used to extend back from all these cottages, particularly on the east side, as far as 'Closes End' by the Recreation Ground.
The THREE TUNS INN has a 1690(?) datestone. The ground floor windows with unusual detached heads are interesting. The inn was probably much damaged in the 1915 Fire. There is a Sun Insurance

fire-mark.

No.24 was the old Post Office and bakery, which was run by Bert and Gwen Taylor until 1970. The long close behind it may now be the only one which runs almost to Closes End. The cottage has an insurance fire-mark.

No.20 has a 1912 datestone. No.17 might have been a shop. There are old shutters on a lower window and unusually the entrance is on the south side.

WHITTALL HOUSE (No.15) appears to be nineteenth-century but there are signs of earlier origins. The house is built of Hornton stone with fine worked joists. There is a long extension at the back. The open porch is twentieth-century.

FERNLEIGH is a brick cottage of the late nineteenth or early twentieth century. George Bevis's sister, Dora, ran a shop here and Morgan's coal yard was next door.

The BUTCHERS ARMS is probably a seventeenth-century building and it may once have comprised two or three dwellings. A butcher and his abattoir used to occupy the space next door.

No.2, on the corner, was originally thatched. It has a Victorian lean-to hood supported on brackets over the six-panel entrance door.

ROSE COTTAGE, opposite, is an old thatched cottage. The gable-end section appears to be older than the lower end, although it is all thatched.

Retrace your steps to Richmond Street.

Richmond Street, formerly Dobbin Street or Dobbin Hoe.

HOME FARM, opposite Blake's Corner, has been the home of the Harper family for over two hundred years. The east block and the south gable, with mullion windows, date from the latter half of the seventeenth century. The west gable-end building is probably an addition, as the walling on the east side is different and older. The south front has two blocked windows. The bay window and the entrance doorway are nineteenth-century. At the rear is the magnificent Great Barn with seven bays. It was once thatched with coped gables and dates from 1680. The datestone high on the west gable is barely legible. Unusually the original steep pitch was kept when the new roof was put on in the 1930s.

SHOEMAKER'S COTTAGE (No.3) is a stone and slate cottage dating from 1683 (see the datestone). In 1856, the Wesleyan Methodists, who had a registered meeting-house in the village from 1820, built a thatched stone chapel behind the cottage for £1370. There used to be signs of the end wall and the old windows of the chapel on the Home Farm side. The 1851 religious census recorded attendance of 15 in the morning and 53 in the afternoon. Later the Methodists here changed their name to The Primitive Methodist Connexion. This chapel served until 1936 when the new Methodist Church was built at the corner of Newlands.

DOBBINS COTTAGE, next door, is a stone and thatched cottage. The east wall shows that it has been much altered and the old wheel might indicate that it was once the home of a wheelwright. It was once the home of Sid Cross, who bought it for £40 in 1928. Earlier it had belonged to the Taylor family.

RICHMOND TERRACE is two cottages end-on to the road, which originally belonged to Home Farm. They have now been converted and the renovations have added half a storey in height. The east wall of these cottages comprises stonework of four different styles, suggesting infill development.

No.15 was built in 1874, as one of four cottages (now three) in Dobbin Street given to the village by Sir William Brown of Astrop House. The brick porches are later additions. No.15 served as a reading-room from 1875 to 1967, when it was sold to buy furniture for the Memorial Hall. One of the other cottages was for the caretaker.

Some of the minutes of the reading-room committee survive. At the first committee meeting on 18 January 1875, the supply of papers was discussed and *The Times, Field, Land & Water,* and *Daily Telegraph* were agreed. Chess, 'Drafts' and Dominoes were alowed (sic) but not any party discussions! Also supplied were the *Illustrated London News, The British Workman, Banbury Guardian, Fun* (later *Punch*), the *Journal of Agriculture* and *Farmers' Chronicle.* A billiard-table and bagatelle board were also available. The minutes also indicate that the period 1887 to 1888 was a time of unemployment and distress, when a soup kitchen was run by some local ladies at the reading-room.

The remainder of Richmond Street is now mainly nineteenth-century stone cottages on the north side, with modern ones on the south side. However, a seventeenth-century painting of the street shows that there was a line of cottages even then on the north side.

Owen Judd by his Chevrolet coal van, with his son Jeffrey and Bill Humphreys on the left, in 1932 (Jeffrey Judd).

Nos.23 and 25 have three very steep gables. The stone arches above the
windows are like those on the barn at Rafters. These were farm-
workers' cottages for Home Farm. Kitchens have been added at the
back.

The old forge used to be where the new bungalow stands next to No.29.
Mr Green, whose wife was a staunch Methodist, was the last blacksmith.

CAVALIER COTTAGE (Nos.29 and 29A) was the home and office of
Owen Judd from 1919, when he moved from Church Farm House in
Fringford. He was a coal merchant and the coal yard was at the rear.
His son, Jeffrey, remembers a Model T Ford lorry and later a 30cwt.
Chevrolet and a two-ton Bedford. In 1941, he made his first journey
collecting coal from the Coventry pits. Owen retired in 1946 due to ill
health and sold the business to Ewart Medley of Adderbury. Jeffrey,
who has lived all his life in the village, built No.14, the modern
bungalow opposite.

No.35, on the corner of Newlands, is under restoration after a serious
fire. Recent examination of the roof structure has revealed that the

building probably dates from c.1580. It has also shown that the building was very cleverly designed to maximise the light in every room. Could it have been used by a weaver?

No.20, opposite, was described in 1615 as the Yew Tree Inn on Dobbin Hoe. The yew tree in the garden could be more than 250 years old. There are attics and cellars inside. The external appearance suggests that it dates from the late eighteenth or early nineteenth century, but internal details support the earlier sixteenth- or seventeenth-century date. The staircase from the first floor to the attics has split balusters like those found in The Court House on the Square.

Round the corner in Newlands there used to be a large stone barn and orchard belonging to George Turvey. He kept his dairy herd here until he sold up and moved to Manor Farm. George is shown as a shopkeeper in 1906 and as a market gardener in 1924. After that he was the village dairyman for many years.

Newlands and the Jitty opposite mark the end of the old village. Take the Jitty for a shorter walk back to Astrop Road.

The JITTY: this is one of the local names given to small passages or alleys e.g. in the Sibfords. Other names include tchure and tuer e.g. in Deddington, Steeple Aston and Upper Heyford, ginnel e.g. in Horley, snicket, twitchell, twitchen, and twitton.

THE OLD CHAPEL (No.37) is now a private house. In 1936, it was built as the Methodist Church to replace the chapel at the rear of Home Farm.

THE SCHOOL, which was built as the County School in 1908, is still open and flourishing. There have been several later additions, the most recent one in the 1970s. In 1931, for the first time the children were allowed to have a midday meal on the premises, heating up food brought from home. In September 1939, more than 100 children arrived as evacuees from Cosway Street School in London. Since 1959 the older children have been attending Brackley Modern School.

OLD SCHOOL HOUSE (No.41) was also built in 1908. There used to be a timber yard on the west side and its office was in the west end of the School House.

BELLE VUE COTTAGES, on the south side, date from 1903, and most of the street here dates from the early twentieth century.

Opposite the Village Stores, there are the remains of an old fish and chip shop, which was just a small wooden shed. The council houses beyond on the left date from the 1950s.

Turn right along The Knob, which leads to "tween towns", the old area between King's Sutton and Astrop, and join Astrop Road.

THE OLD SCHOOL, on the far side, was built as a National School in 1847 on land given by William Willes of Astrop House 'for educating the children of the labouring, manufacturing and other poorer classes in the parish of King's Sutton.' The west end appears to be a later extension. Until 1899, the girls were taught upstairs and the boys downstairs. After 1899, the children were taught in mixed classes but they were still segregated at playtime! The school was closed in 1909 and used as a church hall. It was restored in 1923 into a large hall. It was finally closed in 1964 and later sold to become a private residence.

Walk past the Old School and follow Astrop Road back into King's Sutton.

Prior to 1860, the School and the group of cottages round it were the only dwellings beyond Holland House (No.8). Dolphin Cottage and Hideaway Cottage look to be early buildings. No.28 next to Mistletoe Cottage (No.30) has an 1877 datestone.

ASTROP VILLAS, the four villas on the right, were built c.1890. In 1900, they were still the only cottages on this side of the road until you reach Whittall Street.

HOLLAND HOUSE (No.8), on the left, was built c.1840. There was probably an earlier building on the site which was destroyed in the Great Fire of 1785. The date 1786 is just visible on a stone on the left-hand end at eye-level. The old vicarage, which was pulled down in the 1980s, used to be to the left of Holland House in the present Vicarage Gardens.

THE OLD LACE HOUSE (No.6): in the early 1800s, the Lacemaking School was above this building and the one next door. Children from the age of six used to absent themselves from the Dame school to attend here. The lace-work was mostly pillow lace. The dormer windows and the roof lights mostly date from the early nineteenth century, as does the shop-window.

THE OLD POST OFFICE and STORES was once the Post Office, a

shop and a separate dwelling. The earliest Post Office was run by John Dagley and his wife, and then their daughter, Annie. James McGinlay and his wife took over the Post Office and telephone exchange, which had opened on 25 September 1923. Mrs McGinlay completed the last call on the manual exchange in March 1960, when an automatic exchange replaced the manual one. She was said to listen in to all the telephone calls, so you had to watch what you said! Bert and Gwen Taylor took over the Post Office after the War and ran it at 24 Whittall Street until 1970. Mrs McGinlay retired and closed the shop in 1972. She always kept all her keys on a string at her waist and kept every drawer locked.

Since 1972, little, if anything, has been altered and the old counter and various old jars are visible through the window. It is possible that the old telephone exchange and the old tea drawers, from the time when there were regional tea offices, may still be there. Outside, note the marks of the old letterbox on the wall by the electric water meter.

Return to The Square where we started our walk.

Notes

1 Edwin Walford, *The Pathways of Banburyshire* (1900, revised 1983), 84.

2 Edwin Walford, *The Pathways of Oxfordshire* (1900, revised 1983), 84.

3 Raymond B. Wood-Jones, *Traditional Domestic Architecture in the Banbury Region* (1963), 235-8.

4 Keith Thomas, *Religion and the Decline of Magic* (1971), 543. He also notes the existence of 'witch-posts'.

5 Raymond B. Wood-Jones, *Traditional Domestic Architecture in the Banbury Region*, (1963), 238.

6 Edwin Walford, *The Pathways of Oxfordshire* (1900, reprinted 1983), 84.

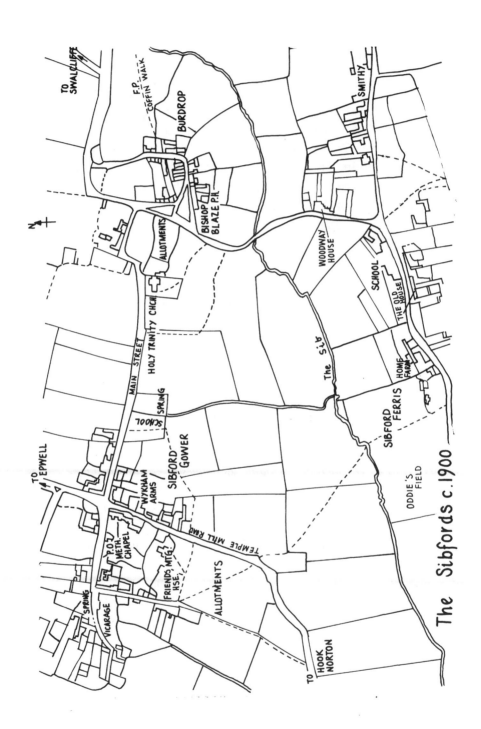

The Sibfords c.1900

Chapter 7

The Sibfords

The twin villages of Sibford Gower and Sibford Ferris are eight miles from Banbury, just off the B4035 Banbury to Shipston-on-Stour road. If you are coming from Banbury, turn left about a mile after Swalcliffe and follow the road into the hamlet of Burdrop and the Sibfords, which stand high on their hilltops. Within living memory, the local inhabitants have called the villages 'Broad Sibbard' (Gower) and 'Little Sibbard' (Ferris).

It is an ancient site and the discovery of flint arrowheads and the remains of two Iron Age barrows are clear links with Ancient Britons who settled here. The settlements were probably chosen for their position and proximity to the nearby ford. In the Domesday survey of 1087, Henry de Ferrieres was noted as the chief landowner at 'Sibforde', which means Sibba's Ford. Gower (Guher) and Ferris are both family names.

In the twelfth century, Robert de Ferrers, the second Earl of Derby, is mentioned in a charter by which William FitzRoger granted nine hides (a hide was between 60 and 180 acres) to the Knights Templar. The Knights Templar were founded c.1119 to protect pilgrims in the Holy Land. They flourished between 1155 and 1312, when they were suppressed by King Philip of France. Temple Close, with its dovecote, and Temple Mill, at the bottom of Woodway Lane, bear witness to the village's Templar connections. There was also a Templar's Chapel in existence c.1150 and it seems to have been preserved until the dissolution of the monasteries. By 1548 it was a ruin and the site is now unknown.[1] About 1560 the Sibford Gower Town Estate was given to the community. The Town Estates Charity is still in existence and nine cottages are let to the poor at a nominal rent.

Sibford Gower was enclosed in 1773, Sibford Ferris in 1789. The 1773 Enclosure Act added ten acres of the former furze land to the Gower Town Estates to be farmed and the profit used to buy fuel for the poor. Unusually it was not until 1840 that the Church of the Holy Trinity in Sibford Gower was built. Until then the Sibfords were included in the Parish of Swalcliffe. In contrast, the Quakers have had a meeting-house on the present site since the seventeenth century. As Leslie Baily commented 'A pioneering or dissenting spirit runs like a silver thread through the history of the Sibford villages and Sibford School.'[2] This spirit is still evident.

From the mid-eighteenth century, plush-weaving was predominant in Banbury. It also provided employment in many surrounding villages, including the Sibfords, Shutford, Swalcliffe and Tadmarton. Shag plush was used for the seats of railway carriages, while Shutford plush was for the livery of Royal servants. Decline began soon after 1840 following the introduction of power looms. The last Banbury plush-making business was bought up in 1908 and the looms taken to Shutford, where the business survived until 1948. Joseph Alcock was the last of the Sibfords' cottage weavers in the 1920s. He used to take his cloth to Shutford where he was paid 11d. a yard.[3]

The populations of both villages peaked in 1851 with 350 in Gower and 549 in Ferris. By 1901, they had declined to 255 and 394 respectively. There were 25 farmers in 1852. By 1887, this had declined to 16 and by 1911 there were only 10. Notable among them have been the Lambs, a Quaker family, who have farmed in the area for over 300 years, living in the Old House in Sibford Ferris for most of that time. Although the population declined significantly in the late nineteenth century, the number of trades shown in the trade directories remained unusually stable at around 25. This had declined to 15 by 1920. By 1991, the population of the twin villages was some 150 less than in 1851 but this has increased recently with the building of new houses. Both villages still have schools and there are public houses in Burdrop and Sibford Gower.

We begin our walk outside the Bishop Blaize Inn in Burdrop (GR 358377).

BURDROP, meaning 'hamlet near the burh' (a town or manor house), was the original hamlet. In the trade directories of 1852 and 1887, three of the gentry and many of the tradesmen in Gower were from Burdrop. The hamlet was clearly a desirable area to live in the mid- to late nineteenth century.

The BISHOP BLAIZE INN was built in 1640 and in 1782 was known as the Old Inn. The first record of the present name is in 1816. Bishop Blaize is the patron saint of wool-combers and there was a wool market on Burdrop Green in the eighteenth century. This is the period when the plush industry was predominant in the Banbury area, so the inn name was probably changed then. The present inn is noted for its good food and warm welcome. There used to be some old cottages by the inn, where a family of Belgian refugees called Poppe lived during the First World War and where Harriet Scruby kept a small shop.

Walk north, straight over the Green, passing cottages on your right, including

BURDROP GREEN with an old mullion window, ENOCK COTTAGE, which was formerly The Little House and later Barthrop Cottage, WYATTS COTTAGE, and WESTSIDE COTTAGE; the last two have old cart entrances.

SHEPHERDS KNOLL was part of a large barn used for storing fleeces before they were sent to market. The barn was converted into three cottages in 1815 but is now one dwelling.

BANK HOUSE is now a large house but may once have been a number of cottages. You can see the outline of an old bread oven on the left-hand end, although it is very overgrown now.

On reaching the main road, turn right along Hawkes Lane and after 100 yards take the gravel public footpath (The Jitty) on the right, opposite The Cubbs. At the end of the path, turn right past the surgery.

NICHOLAS CORNER, on the left, has two very old windows, one of them flanked by two gargoyles. There is an older part of the building at the rear. A doctor used to live here. There is a row of old thatched cottages opposite, and one of them has the date 1724 above the door. There used to be a reading-room in one of them.

On the left, note the narrow public footpath.

COFFIN WALK is also known as Dead Man's Walk. This was the route taken by coffin bearers to funerals at Swalcliffe Church, since there was no church in the Sibfords until 1840. This direct walk avoided the natural swamp in Hawkes Lane.

BURDROP HOUSE, on the left, is a substantial three-storey farm-house, probably dating from the eighteenth century. Another doctor used to live here.

The RED HOUSE next door, and BRAYES CLOSE on the right, are

Hill into Sibford Ferris, with Woodway House and Pettifers Place, 1920s (OCC). (OCL76/48).

both built of brick, first used in the Sibfords c.1805. Some of the earliest brick in Oxfordshire was used at Hanwell Castle, where it was made on site at the beginning of the seventeenth century.

On your right, after the right hand bend, you can see:

The WATER POINT, an old tap with a brick surround. There is a 312-gallon tank behind this water point, which was fed by a hydraulic ram from Holywell below the churchyard. It was installed in 1847 at a cost of £50, funded by public subscription. William Fox from Sibford Gower built the ram and some forty others elsewhere, as far afield as Kent.

CARRIERS COTTAGE, opposite, used to have a bakery behind. 'Cuckoo' Jim Stowe lived here when he was the gamekeeper at Weston Park near Whichford. He was noted for imitating the cuckoo some weeks before the cuckoo arrived and so fooling the village – until they got wise to him! He knew everything about snaring animals.

Carriers were going to Banbury from c.1811, mainly to The Waggon and Horses (now Banbury Cross) in Butchers Row/Shambles. This meant a

The first Sibford taxi, a Model T Ford, driven by a stylish Mrs May Jarvis, in 1916 (Arnold Lamb).

three-hour journey each way, two or three days a week. The Lines family from Sibford Ferris were carriers more or less continuously from c.1864 to 1906.

Walk down the hill across the Sib and up the very steep hill into Sibford Ferris.

The Sib rises east of the village and joins the Stour at Temple Mill. These streams are unique in Oxfordshire as they run west into the Avon/Severn and not east into the Thames and North Sea.

George Dyer owned the cowshed on the hill on the left. The Dyers lived in the farm at the top of the hill and George used to supply milk to Sibford School, carrying two 5-gallon churns on a yoke.

WOODWAY HOUSE, on the left, is an old farmhouse, which has been much altered, with some shocking bay window extensions. Joseph Pettifer, a major landowner and 'breeder of high class fancy poultry', was living here in 1899. PETTIFER'S PIECE next door was formerly a barn and stable.

MARIA'S HOUSE is named after Maria Payne, a servant of Susanna Farden, who kept a post office, then a wool shop. Maria was a staunch Quaker and supporter of Sibford School. There used to be two cottages on the grass area in front. In the seventeenth century the end part, which clearly used to be thatched, was Jeremiah Lamb's smithy.

Look over the wall into the valley.

There the depressions indicate the position of medieval fish-ponds, which used to supply fish to the old manor. Today these depressions are liable to flooding.

Sibford School, 1920s (OCC).

Walk on to the crossroads. If you walk up the road to the left, note

MALVERN HOUSE, on the left, which used to be the doctor's house.
   There is a fine garden and rockery behind, dating from c.1900.
   Green's, the village shop, is just beyond, and there used to be a
   smithy a little further up the road.

Return to the crossroads.

SIBFORD SCHOOL, originally The Society of Friends School, used to
   be in the old Manor House on the right. In 1839, there was a move to
   establish an agricultural school in the Midlands. By 1841 a site had
   been agreed and Joshua Lamb organised the purchase of the Manor
   House for the Quakers. The cost was £1200 and it was bought for the
   'purpose of having a school'. The extensions to the right were built at
   this time. The northern face of the building may date from the
   sixteenth century, although Thomas Walford probably carried out
   some major rebuilding work on the 'Great House', as it was locally

known, in 1666. The major transformation occurred in the early eighteenth century, when the Walfords restyled the building in the Queen Anne fashion.

Gardners Directory of 1852 states 'Besides usual rudiments of an English education the boys are instructed in the science of agriculture & the girls are taught the domestic duties'. Previously, in the early 1800s, there had been a Quaker day-school in the Manor.[4] The whole school is now up the hill opposite, where the first school building was opened in 1930. The original school site has been developed to provide nineteen units and the old Manor House has been converted into flats.

HOME CLOSE, a long and low two-storeyed house on the left, was designed in 1911 by H.Baillie Scott, in the traditional Cotswold style and completed in 1912. There used to be a barn next door where the Lambs kept their pigs. There is a large long garden behind, stretching up to Bank Lane. Mr Hiles, who was the first owner and an artist, also owned and supported the reading-room, which was part of the modern Westerways.

The OLD BAKEHOUSE is probably older than the sixteenth-century Old House next door. It was the first Post Office in the village in the 1890s. There is a stream running through the cellar, and you can see the outlet on the roadside which has now been capped.

The OLD HOUSE probably dates from the sixteenth century. Generations of the Lamb family, who have farmed in the area for over three centuries, have lived in this house continuously since 1658, apart from a short period of about ten years! The house is virtually unaltered, with the exception of the right-hand end. This used to be the washhouse and has now been converted into a separate cottage. The beehive-shaped building by the roadside was the Lambs' summer house, where the family photos used to be taken. One of the outbuildings on the roadside was the toilet which used to seep onto the road near to the spring outlet! You can still see the arched stones above the outlet at road level. There used to be two other similar springs on this stretch of Main Street.

The most eccentric member of the family was Theodore Lamb, the Hermit, who was born in 1880. He was educated at Sibford School and became a skilled repairer of watches and locks. He lived in Bond's End Lane for a while but moved out to The Heath, where he lived as a hermit for forty years. He was well known in the area and

The Lamb family moving house in Sibford Ferris c.1916. No vans for hire then! (Arnold Lamb).

was never without his moneybag, charging a penny to have his picture taken and always collecting 'for meself'. There are many stories about him, for example, how he rode a tyreless bicycle, ate raw eggs and wore revealing clothes made of sackcloth. However, he lived the way he wanted and was well respected by many.

YEW TREE COTTAGE probably dates from the late eighteenth century. It was originally three cottages of unusual design, each being two-storey, with one room on each floor. Two fossils, which were unearthed here in 1986, have been identified as bivalves from the Jurassic Period, about 180 million years ago!

WESTERWAYS was a wheelwright's cottage. There was a meeting-room here, which was used by the Home Guard during the Second World War. The village reading-room also used to be on this site. It was a very busy place between the Wars, open every evening from 6.00 to 9.30pm and providing facilities for all sorts of games. It closed when the War started. Next door you can still see the window of the saddler's shop.

Across the main road on the right, you can see:

HOME FARM: all the area to the right of the old farm used to be occupied by the outbuildings and farmyard. They were converted some

Theodore Lamb on Sibford Heath, off the Brailes road, 1920s. Note his money-bag with which he was always collecting 'for meself' (OCC).

twenty years ago, when the extension on the right of the farmhouse was built.

WEST TOWN COTTAGE, next to Home Farm, has an old mullion window on the west gable and other old windows.

Take the footpath on the right down the hill across Oddie's Field.

ODDIE'S FIELD is named after Robert Oddie, a farmer and head-master of Sibford School in the late nineteenth century. Hugh Oddie, his grandson, was a pilot, who was killed in 1943, and there is a window dedicated to him in the church. The undulating nature of the field was created by clay-digging in the late 1700s to form bricks and tiles for West Town House. The large hole in the western half (much filled in later) was the site of the kiln. Poulton was the brickmaker and there is some doubt whether he had the right to dig up the field!

At the bottom, cross the Sib, then follow the path diagonally up the hill over a stile into Sycamore Close and Temple Mill Road; turn right and note the large house on the right.

TEMPLE CLOSE, which used to be called Norton House, has a lovely garden. It was one of many properties owned by Frank Lascelles. The name of the house indicates the village's connection with the Knights Templar. The west end was originally two old cottages and there is a dovecote in the roadside building. Wheelwrights used to live here. At the rear there is a blocked window and some mullion windows in the older east end.

Take the footpath opposite.

The present SOCIETY OF FRIENDS MEETING HOUSE dates from 1864, as the datestone indicates. There has been a meeting-house on this site since 1681, when a small building was erected by a band of Puritans, following a visit in 1678 from George Fox, the Quaker leader. Until the Methodist Chapel was completed in 1827, this seems to have been the only place of worship in the Sibfords. The 1851 religious census recorded attendance of 112 at morning service. Inside the meeting-house there used to be a partition, which could be lowered to separate men and women. Some of the panels from it were used in building the Mission Room next door in 1890.

Take the path across the graveyard to another footpath. Turn right and walk to the end of the path.

Bond's End Lane

The lane, which is shown on an early map as Bones End Lane, was a tradesmen's area, home to a number of plush outworkers, including Joseph Alcock, who was the last plush-weaver in the Sibfords in the 1920s. There were also a number of small shops until the early 1960s when the last one closed. Theodore Lamb lived here before he moved out to The Heath.

LEASOWE, the large house at the bottom of the lane, was formerly Innisfree. In the late nineteenth century, a Dame school was run in the brick building next door by the three Misses Shemeld, who were Quakers. It closed sometime before the First World War. The row of brick cottages next door was probably connected to Leasowe and may have been built by the local Enoch brothers.

As you walk up the lane, note the following:

Sibford Gower village pond with T.E. Griffin's horse and cart, 1930s. Griffin was the Epwell baker who delivered regularly to the Sibfords. Note the stone well-head, covering 'Town Well', which was erected by John Gilkes on 9 October 1845 (OCC).

a) BRAMLEY CLOSE, on the right: Alfred Stowe and his wife used to have a small market garden and a little shop here.

b) QUINCE COTTAGE and other old cottages on the left, and BAKE-HOUSE COTTAGE at the top end on the right. Given the limited space, the gable-end of a number of the cottages fronts onto the lane.

As you enter Main Street, turn left. You are now in the old part of Sibford Gower.

The OLD VICARAGE, on the corner, was given by the Wykeham family of Swalcliffe Manor in the 1650s for use by the vicars, who lived here until the 1970s. The seventeenth-century farm comprised the small building to the right, with the barn beyond it. The main house is probably eighteenth-century. Note the false window painted on the first floor level above the porch.

TOWN WELL: in front of the Old Vicarage, note the stone well-head which was erected by John Gilkes on 9 October 1845. The well is fed from the pond and is still functional today.

The VILLAGE POND opposite was fed by local springs for centuries. It used to overflow across the village track until 1900 when it was kerbed and the ford piped. The large chestnut tree was raised from a conker, picked up beside the body of Joseph John Lamb. In 1887, he fell and broke his neck while knocking down conkers for his seven-year old son in Oddie's Field. Eric Payne and his father both worked for another member of the Lamb family, John, who owned Elmridge Farm behind the pond.

Turn back up Main Street towards the crossroads.

CEDARHOLME on the corner of Bond's End Lane has been the home of Eric Payne since 1946. He and his wife ran the Post Office from 1959 to 1979 and Eric has been a churchwarden for over 40 years. Eric, his father, and grandfather all worked on the land in the Sibfords and his uncle was the local pigsticker. His mother was a good friend of Frank Lascelles at The Manor and Eric met Ivor Novello there. Old Mrs Moore lived at Cedarholme before the Paynes. She was convinced that there was a ghost 'that stands at the end of the bed', which used to take her needle and thread and return it some days later!

The OLD POST OFFICE, on the right by the telephone kiosk, was originally owned and run as a Post Office by the Inns family, starting in 1884. Frederick Inns, who ran it from then until the 1930s, was also a plumber and glazier and would turn his hand to anything. The Paynes took over in 1959. In the early twentieth century, when there were three bands in the village, the string band used to rehearse here. One brass band rehearsed at the Bishop Blaize Inn and another one, a Temperance Band, at the Quaker Mission Room. There was once another shop next door in IVY COTTAGE.

Opposite the Post Office, on the left of Tamlet Cottage (datestone STG 1765(?)), a steep footpath provides a short detour, where on the left an old dovecote can just be seen. It appears to be sixteenth-century and belonged to the ancient manor. Return to Main Street and note some of the other old houses, seventeenth-century or earlier, as you walk towards the crossroads.

YEW TREE HOUSE, on the right, with an eighteenth-century façade, was the old manor. The doorknockers are the same as those on The

Manor, as Frank Lascelles had them copied.

WEST FARM COTTAGE is opposite, and beyond it THE MOUNT and BARNES COTTAGE. At the crossroads, there are two brick cottages, where Mr Eden, a policeman, lived in the top one with his nine children!

CARTERS YARD, on the corner opposite, is a seventeenth-century house, which was destroyed by fire c.1929 when a spark from a passing steam engine set fire to it.

Turn right down Temple Mill Road.

The WESLEYAN METHODIST CHAPEL, on the right, was built in 1827 and rebuilt in 1864. Attendance in 1851 was 100 in the afternoon and 90 in the evening. In 1927, centenary services, attended by over 200, were held in the Friends Meeting House – evidence of friendly relations between the different faiths.

THE WYKHAM ARMS, opposite, is of uncertain date but a penny of 1537 was found here in the 1950s. Some of the buildings at the rear are still thatched. The inn was (despite the spelling) no doubt named after the Wykehams of Swalcliffe Manor, who built part of Swalcliffe Church in the fourteenth century and the famous Tithe Barn in the fifteenth century.

The old village hall used to stand behind the inn. Frank Lascelles bought a large army hut after the First World War and presented it to the village. It was large enough for dances. After Lascelles died in 1954, the hall was repossessed to help pay his debts but the villagers were quick enough to rescue the contents before repossession.

The MANOR HOUSE, on the right, formerly The Cottage, was the home of Frank Lascelles (1875-1954), Pageant Master of the Oxford Historical Pageant of 1910 and the British Empire Pageant of 1924. He also created pageants in Calcutta, Canada, and elsewhere. He bought the Lordship from Christ Church, Oxford in 1915 for £3,100 and the manor for a further £10. He may have inherited an old cottage on the site from his nanny. He remodelled the manor c.1915 by linking and extending several seventeenth-century cottages and an old barn 'into a riotous nightmare of the picturesque, thatched and wildly irregular, with a stone tower and brick flying buttresses'.[5] Note the old mullion window low down in the centre.

Lascelles was born Frank Stevens, son of the rector, but he used many

The Manor, Sibford Gower, with Frank Lascelles and possibly his sister, Rosa, in the doorway, 1920s. The car is a Standard (c.1907) (OCC).

names. As well as being a Pageant Master, he was a talented actor, sculptor, and artist, and a very colourful character, who spent hugely and died with large debts. He always wore a long flowing blue cloak and he used to take some of the boys after school for a ride in his carriage, drawn by four cream horses. Ivor Novello was among many artistic visitors and he is said to have composed 'Keep the Home Fires Burning' here in 1914.

The MEETING HOUSE COTTAGE AND MISSION ROOM were built c.1890 and some of the panels from the Meeting House were used. The Mission Room is still used occasionally. It is very plain, as you would expect, but used to have a much higher ceiling. The cottage was for the caretaker.

BUTTSLADE HOUSE, opposite the Mission Room, used to be a farm with a Jersey herd which supplied the village with milk. Note the old mounting block at the front. The south end seems to be a newer extension. Arrow-shooting used to be practised here, hence the reference to the Butts.

Take the footpath on the left, noting the rear of Temple Close. After crossing a stile, take a short detour to the right to see The Tite.

THE TITE: a spring feeds the pool and has provided fresh water to the village for centuries. It was used by the villagers until mains water came in 1935/36.

Continue on the footpath up the hill to the School on the right.

The ENDOWED PRIMARY SCHOOL, which dates from 1623, was an Endowed National School and later became an Elementary School. The present main building dates from 1866. By 1900, a new classroom was added and up to 100 children attended the school. In 1961, major alterations were carried out, including a new hall and the conversion of two classrooms. In 1968, the 'New School' was built across the road, producing a split-site arrangement. Since then further extensions and improvements have been completed on both sides of the road.

The original endowment came from the Town Estate, given in 1560, and it allowed Gower and Ferris children to be educated free. Canon Edward Payne, vicar of Swalcliffe (1837-86), describes as follows the provision for education in his large parish, when he first succeeded to the living: 'As to schools, nothing beyond a very primitive dame's school existed anywhere in either Parish except at Sibford Gower, where there was an endowed mixed school, supported by what ought to have been a wealthy charity, but which had been badly managed for many years and was encumbered by heavy debt. Moreover the Schoolmaster was a broken down Wool Stapler who had been appointed to the office in order to save his parish pay, whilst his wife, though each and all of the three R's was utterly beyond her, officiated as School Mistress. The school buildings were ruinous.'[6]!

Turn left on Main Street and note

SCHOOL HOUSE opposite and THE OLD CO-OP just beyond it.
GOWER CLOSE and THE COURT HOUSE, on the left, are both seventeenth-century or earlier, as are the cottages opposite. The Sabin family, who were carriers, lived in the Close, where they had stables for their horses. Sibford Gower held its own medieval court, free of other jurisdiction, because of its connection to the Knights Templar.

Turn back past the school alomg Acre Ditch towards the church.

Sibford Fete, 10 August 1909, with the Barford Merry- go-round, on the site of the present village hall which was built in 1957 (OCC).

The CHURCH OF THE HOLY TRINITY was not built until 1840, so that the Sibford Anglicans were part of Swalcliffe Parish until then. The church is unusual in having neither a tower nor a steeple, and in being built in a Greek cross design, with a short chancel, nave and transepts, all of equal width and height, meeting in a great wide crossing. In 1897, a new porch was built in memory of Miss Elizabeth Dix.

In the south transept there is a lovely memorial to his mother sculpted by Frank Lascelles. This has been described as 'the face of an old lady of tender grace looking out of a bower of roses'. The organ and choir stalls date from 1906 when they were built by public subscription. The window on the north side is dedicated to the Revd William Sanderson Miller (vicar 1848-60), and a window on the south side to three members of the Pettipher family. There is also a window dedicated to Flying Officer Hugh Oddie, a grandson of Robert Oddie, headmaster of Sibford School, who was killed in 1943.

SIBFORD HALL, the village hall opposite, was built in 1957. Lewis

Poulton, who lived in Burdrop Farm House, used to own this land. Cricket used to be played behind the Hall.

'Beyond the End', on the gate next to the church, must mark the end of Sibford Gower and the start of Burdrop. On the next corner, note Burdrop Farm House, with an old barn and a number of new houses converted from farm buildings.

Take the footpath on the right by Park End Farm, which leads back to the Bishop Blaize Inn.

Notes

1   Leslie Baily, *From the Romans to Rock-N-Roll* (1960), 8-11.
2   Leslie Baily, quoted by M.R.Finch in *From Manor House to Quaker School* (1997), 4.
3   Leslie Baily, *From the Romans to Rock-N-Roll* (1960),12.
4   M.R. Finch, *From Manor House to Quaker School*, 5.
5   Sherwood & Pevsner, *The Buildings of England: Oxfordshire* (1974), 767.
6   Diana McClatchey, *Oxfordshire Clergy 1777-1869* (1960), 155.

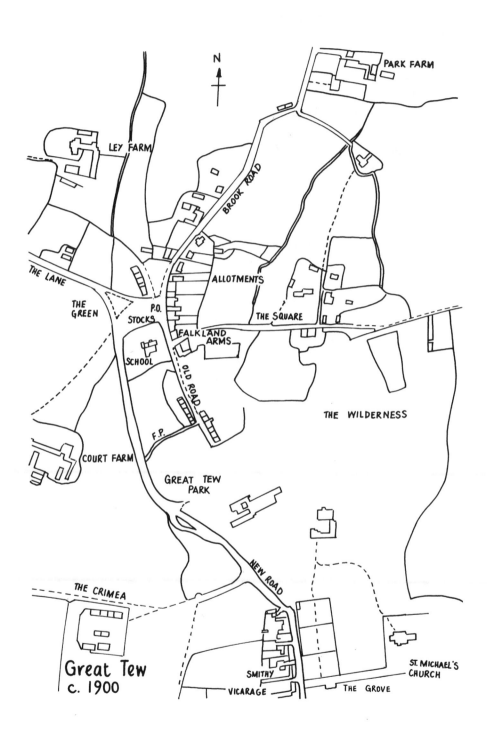

N

PARK FARM

LEY FARM

BROOK ROAD

THE LANE

ALLOTMENTS

THE GREEN

P.O.
STOCKS

THE SQUARE

FALKLAND ARMS

SCHOOL

OLD ROAD

THE WILDERNESS

F.P.

COURT FARM

GREAT TEW PARK

NEW ROAD

THE CRIMEA

Great Tew
c. 1900

SMITHY

VICARAGE

THE GROVE

St. MICHAEL'S CHURCH

Chapter 8

Great Tew

Great Tew, a famously attractive village with the renowned Falkland Arms, is nine miles from Banbury and six miles from Chipping Norton and can be reached off the B4031 road to Deddington. Tew may refer to a 'long ridge'. The Anglo-Saxon form 'Church Tew' reflected its importance as an early ecclesiastical centre. Neighbouring Duns Tew may have formed part of the same estate, as the road running west from there was called Churchway. Beaconsfield Farm, to the south of the village, was an important Roman site in the third and fourth centuries. Parliamentary enclosure was completed in 1767, following partial enclosure in 1622 by Sir Lawrence Tanfield. He was Chief Baron of the Exchequer and grandfather of Lucius Cary, the 2nd Viscount Falkland, with whom the village is always associated.

Lucius Cary (1609-43) is famous for his part in the Civil War, during which he was a leading member of the Circle at Tew, a group of advisers to Charles I, and a forceful advocate of a peaceful solution to the war. He was killed at the first battle of Newbury on 23 September 1643. Lucius' widow, Lettice, and then his sons, held the estate until 1694. The Earl of Clarendon has left a lasting memorial to him in his wonderful description of the meetings of the Circle at Tew, where writers and scholars 'resorted and dwelt with him as in a College situated in a purer air'. This description and his elegy on the death of Lord Falkland, which is one of the most famous in English literature, both deserve to be quoted more fully:

The Circle at Tew[1]

'His house… looked like the university itself, by the company that was always found there. These were Dr Sheldon, Dr Morley, Dr Hammond, Dr Earles, Mr Chillingworth, and indeed all men of eminent parts, and faculties in Oxford, besides those who resorted thither from London, who all found lodgings there, as ready as in the colleges; nor did the lord of the house know of their coming and going, nor who were in the house, till he

Tew Park south front, 1930s (OCC).

came to dinner, or supper, where all still met; otherwise, there was no troublesome ceremony or constraint, to forbid men to come to the house, or make them weary of staying there; so that many came thither to study in a better air, finding all the books that they could desire in his library, and all the persons together, whose company they could wish, and not find in any other society.'

Elegy on the Death of Lucius Cary, the second Lord Falkland[2]

'... a loss which no time will suffer to be forgotten, and no success or good fortune could repair. In this unhappy battle was slain the lord viscount Falkland; a person of such prodigious parts of learning and knowledge, of that inimitable sweetness and delight in conversation, of so flowing and obliging a humanity and goodness to mankind, and of that primitive simplicity and integrity of life, that if there were no other brand upon this odious and accursed civil war than that single loss, it must be most infamous and execrable to all posterity.'

Tew Park

The village has been dominated by Tew Park and its owners since the sixteenth century. The Park was created in the years 1550 to 1580 and the

Old Road was diverted round the site. The old E-shaped manor was built from 1575 to 1610, with the main front facing south, a walled garden on the west, and the church to the east. Lucius Cary made significant additions to this house but only the garden walls, which form three large enclosures, survive. In 1611, Sir Lawrence Tanfield bought the estate from Edward Rainsford, and in 1622 he enclosed part of the village. By then almost all the village was in single ownership. There were many complaints about Tanfield and his wife, Elizabeth, who was accused of saying that the villagers were 'more worthy to be ground to powder than to have any favour showed to them'! Tanfield's ghost is said to drive a coach and six round Tew Park. In 1698, Francis Keck purchased the estate. When he died in 1728, it was said that he was 'the richest man and had the best estate... in Oxfordshire'.[3] His nephew, John Tracy, took the estate and the name of Keck.

By 1750, a tree-lined avenue had been planted by Keck running over a mile to the north end of South Newington; another avenue, half a mile long, connected it to the Manor. The northern end of the avenue was destroyed by J.C. Loudon. In the period 1800 to 1814, G.F. Stratton bought out most of the tenants and in 1808 appointed J.C. Loudon to set up an experimental farm on the lines of Scottish 'convertible husbandry'. At times in this period as many as 130 men were working on the improvements. Not surprisingly this over-ambitious experiment failed. Loudon departed in 1811 and he later admitted that it would be remembered as 'a ruinous project of wild adventurers'.[4]

In 1815, M.R. Boulton, son of the famous Birmingham engineer, Matthew (1728-1809), bought the estate from Stratton. His father had been partner with James Watt in the Soho Engineering Works and assisted him in the introduction of the steam engine. From 1816 to 1844, M.R. Boulton undertook the rebuilding of Great Tew in a very 'ornamental and singular style'. The bulk of the early expenditure was on the mansion house and some of the farms, notably Tracey and Beaconsfield to the south of the village, and Park Farm on the north side. There was also great tree planting. The core of the new house was a small Georgian dower house, to the east of which a Gothic library was added c.1825. In 1842, M.R. Boulton was succeeded by his son, M.P.W. Boulton.

From 1850 to 1856 there was a second phase of rebuilding, when the village took on its present day shape. Road closures divided the village into three or four apparently unrelated groups of cottages. Main Street (the Old Road to The Green), which ran up to the Manor, was cut off by the new

Park boundary and the New Road was created west of the Manor, running down past the Green to The Lane. The rebuilding included a brickyard north-west of Hookerswell Farm, south of the village. In 1856, a Tudor extension was built west of the dower house. From 1868 to 1872 there was further heavy expenditure, the additions including the large kitchen garden south of the Ledwell Road.

In 1914, the unmarried M.E. Boulton died, and his estate was administered by the Public Trustee, which led to a decline in its fortunes. His sisters, Clara and Margaret, had successive life interests, since Matthew, his brother and last male heir, was killed in the trenches. The sisters rarely walked through the village and when they did in the 1920s 'life almost came to a standstill, men touching their caps or forelocks, women curtseying, and the children following suit.'[5] In 1962, Major Eustace Robb, grandson of Mary Ann Boulton (MPW's sister), inherited the estate but he had been living in the Manor since 1952. In 1985, the estate passed to James Johnston, Robb's agent and partner, and to his son, Nicholas, who now runs it.

The Village

Enclosure was completed in 1767, when the major beneficiary was Anthony Keck (1,457 acres). In 1801, the population was 402. By 1851, the population had grown to a peak of 541 and by 1876 Great Tew was 'one of the best farmed parishes in the Midland counties'. By 1901, the population had fallen to 334, and by 1991 it was down to 147. There are only two tenant farmers now, where there were once fourteen. For much of the nineteenth century the Barlows were at Park Farm, the Nevilles at Court Farm, and the Kimbers at Tracey Farm. For much of the twentieth century, the Louch family were at Court Farm and the Tustians at Hookerswell, The Leys, and Upper Park Farms. There were regular carriers to Banbury from 1796. Hubert Keal and then his son, Charles, were the carriers from c.1900 to the 1930s. They used to go to the Catherine Wheel in Cow Fair two or three times a week, and to Chipping Norton on Wednesdays.

In 1876, unusually, both the publican and carpenter were women, Mrs Spencer at The Falkland Arms and Mrs Shelton the carpenter. In 1899, two of the farmers were women, Mrs Caroline Gregory and Mrs Catherine Hollis, and Mrs Laura Shelton was the carpenter. In 1915, she was still the carpenter and by 1924 the family tradition was being carried on by Charlie Shelton, who could 'claim the prize for versatility'. Apart from being the village carpenter and wheelwright, he was the sexton, an efficient bell-ringer, and a general handyman, whose skills included the mending of bicycles and the shoeing of horses when business was too brisk for the blacksmith.[6] There was also continuity at the Post Office and the little shop on the Green. In 1911, Miss Florence Chedzey was sub-postmistress and Thomas Gregory was the shopkeeper. By 1924 Miss Ada Gregory had taken over the Little Handy Shop on the Green, which she ran until 1945. Florence Chedzey continued at the Post Office with Miss Parrot until the Second World War.

By 1977 the village was in danger of crumbling away and in 1978 it was declared a Conservation Area. Even in 1986 it was still in 'romantic decay', because tenants were paying peppercorn rents and the estate had little money for maintenance. In the early 1980s, 23 houses were sold, 25 were restored and let, and 15 were let on 'friendly terms' to artisans e.g. architects, artists, designers, and thatchers. Some tenants continued to live rent-free in tied cottages. Under the Johnstons, there is a continuing programme of refurbishment. Recent work has included restoration of a number of houses on The Square and opening up the view of the Manor from New Road.

We begin our walk at the gateway to the churchyard, opposite the Vicarage (GR 398288).

The gateway, which may have been moved from Lucius Cary's old mansion, may date from c.1632. On the lintel note that two swags of flowers have been re-set upside down! The gateway was restored in 1992 in memory of Eustace Robb (see the plaque).

THE GROVE is on the right as you walk towards the church. On the left are the walled gardens of Tew Park. The Grove was well established by 1767 thanks to John Keck, who ran the estate from 1728 to 1778. It was there that the "Tew Tree" stood, a giant silver fir providing a landmark for much of the nineteenth century.

ST MICHAEL AND ALL ANGELS CHURCH: enjoy the sheer magic of this secluded church, the lightness of the interior, and on no account miss the beautiful tomb of Mary Anne Boulton sculpted by Sir Francis Chantrey. The church is built chiefly in the Decorated style c.1300. The south doorway is late Norman from c.1170, while the porch is Early English of the thirteenth century. Note the rare use of dark and light stone in the surrounding archway and on the south

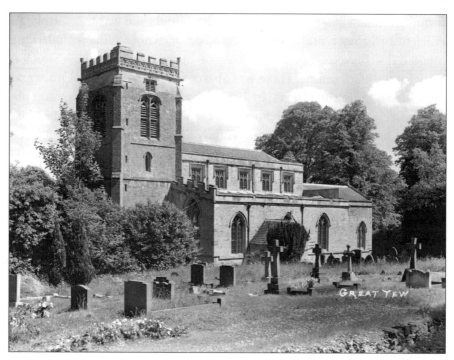

St Michael and All Angels Church, 1930s (OCC).

wall of the chancel.

14th century: the aisles were widened, a new chancel arch was inserted and the chancel was largely rebuilt. Some traces of wall paintings in the south aisle and on the west wall of the north aisle were uncovered in 1988 and may date from c.1300. In the vestry there is the early fourteenth-century stone effigy of a knight in chain armour with aiguillettes (or aglets); he is believed to be Robert de Vere, a Great Tew landowner. He is one of only four similar effigies now remaining in England with these defensive pieces.

15th century: the lower stages of the tower were built c.1400 and the very fine font is from this period. The upper stages of the tower were built at the end of the century, with the clerestory, nave, the aisle roofs and parapets.

19th century: from 1826 to 1827 Thomas Rickman repaired the church and chancel, and also the vicarage. Note the fine corbels on the nave ceiling. The unusual three-decker pulpit, with a reading desk and clerk's desk, dates from the early part of that century. The box pews in the south aisle were made for the estate servants. In 1830, M.R. Boulton referred to the Revd Samuel Nash (vicar 1790-1829) as the 'late, insane incumbent' and alleged that for twenty years the parish had been deprived of 'all efficient pastoral superintendance'.[7]

Tombs and memorials

a) On the south wall of the chancel, there is a memorial to Lucius Cary, which was erected by M.P.W.Boulton in 1885.

c) In the chancel, there is a beautifully sculpted tomb to Mary Anne Boulton, Matthew's wife, by Sir Francis Chantrey (1781-1841). The lovely reclining figure is sitting with a book which has slipped from her hand while she looks away lost in a dream. It is signed and dated 1834.

Nonconformists

From the late eighteenth century, neighbouring Little Tew was a fertile centre for nonconformity in the wider parish. Its Baptist Chapel was built in 1845 and in 1851 morning attendance was 117. Surprisingly, there were also significant numbers of nonconformists in Great Tew, which you might expect to be a 'closed' village. In 1854, the vicar reported that one-third of the villagers were Baptists or Ranters i.e. Primitive Methodists. In 1869, an estimated 150 Primitive Methodists were attending meetings in a cottage – it must have been a very large one! In 1878, there were still some 30 nonconformist families but there is no evidence of a chapel being built in Great Tew.

Retrace your steps to New Road.

THE VICARAGE opposite was the home of George Stratton, who acquired the whole estate c.1790. There is a 1781 datestone on one side but the rest of the house is much older, with a datestone of 1696 on the north side. There were major alterations in 1829 by Thomas Rickman, who restored the church.

45-49 NEW ROAD: this row of houses, facing the walled garden, was built between 1675 and 1696. The Forge Cottage Workshop is in the middle. Note the old wide gateway for carts. The last blacksmith was Jack Gibbard, who worked here until c.1950.

6 NEW ROAD, on the left, was probably an eighteenth-century cottage, although the 1728 datestone may be one of several placed during the nineteenth-century rebuilding.

THE CRIMEA YARD, on the left along the Old Norton Way: the 1856 buildings in the Yard are dominated by the tall chimney of the old

Charles Linzey, on the Ledwell Road, bringing in the horses to Court Farm where he worked for James Louch, 1920s (Violet Kench).

sawmill's engine-house, which was still working in the 1930s. Cherry and Sons, the builders, moved here from Cropredy in 2000. There is one old derelict cottage remaining on the south side.

THE ESTATE OFFICE, on New Road, comprises an old house and a new office building.

TEW PARK: the entrance to the park, to which there is no public access, is down on the right. There is now a fine view of the Manor and the houses below. To the left on the hill you can see Court Farm, home of the Nevilles in the nineteenth century and the Louch family for much of the twentieth century.

Take a small fenced footpath on the right, down to the houses on Old Road.

OLD ROAD: to the right the road is cut off by the Park boundary but there is now a fine view of the north front of the Manor. The row of thatched cottages here is sixteenth- and seventeenth-century, with mullion windows:

a) Nos. 8-11 to the right: No.10 has an old through-passage next to the front door.

The Old Road looking towards Tew Park in 1929 (OCC).

b) No.12 has a 1636 datestone by the lintel, the arms of the Falkland
   family, and an old sundial. These were all reset during the nineteenth-
   century improvements.

c) As you walk towards the Falkland Arms, note No.15 and Lily and
   Bluebell cottages on the south side.

Take the path by the Falkland Arms past Hornbeam House to The Square.

THE SQUARE has a fine collection of seventeenth-century cottages
   round a small Green. These were derelict in the 1970s but most of
   them have now been restored.

a) No.56, below on the left, was built in 1680 by John Hiorn for John
   Stowe. There is a fine cellar with a recess, possibly for a fire, although
   there is no surviving chimney. There is also a fine old outbuilding.

b) No.49, at the top, is largely unchanged. The horseshoes on the wall
   do not indicate that this was the old smithy: Pratt, the coal merchant,
   lived here.

The path beyond leads past The Wilderness and Tew Park. There were
   plans for a playground for children along here, in an area known as
   The Dog Kennel, but the fence was pulled up for firewood before it
   could be made!

The Green with old cottages, c. 1935, including The Little Handy Shop (No.44) run by Ada Gregory. The lady may be Dolly Morley (née Kench) who lived on the Green (OCC).

Turn left and take the path down across the field. Cross the stream and take the track past Brookside to Brook Road.

The road to the right leads to the Chipping Norton road, past LOWER PARK FARM, formerly Park Farm, where the Barlows lived for most of the nineteenth century.

Turn left up the hill.

BEE BOLE COTTAGE (Nos.36 and 37) is a stone and wooden struc-ture. Local tradition has it that the row of low gothic arches, standing in the garden, was built c.1856 to house beehives.

TULIP TREE HOUSE is one of the few surviving eighteenth-century houses and it has been restored from a semi-derelict state. Note the wooden mullioned and transomed windows, and the stone slate roof with dormers. There is a fine large garden and some old stables below. One of the large Tustian clan used to live here.

BANKSIDE (No.31), on the left, is a tall thatched ashlar cottage, reput-edly built for the estate foreman in the period from 1850 to 1856.

As you progress up the hill towards The Green, note the gable-end

The Falkland Arms with Mr Prattley sitting on the Stocks, 1960s (OCC).

cottage of the seventeenth or eighteenth century on the left, and the seventeenth-century Porch House, with a two-storey porch.

THE GREEN: many of the cottages here are seventeenth-century. The Little Handy Shop (No.44) was run by Miss Ada Gregory from the 1920s to 1945. Little Thatch (No.43) has been extended and No.41 below is about to be. Note the fine stone porch of No.47.

THE FALKLAND ARMS: the inn and the terrace of cottages date from the seventeenth and eighteenth centuries. In the period 1700 to 1815 there were two inns, The Pole Axe run by the Adams family, and The Horse and Groom, which by the 1830s was called The Falkland Arms. For much of the eighteenth century it was run by the Worley family.

THE ENDOWED SCHOOL (MIXED) and MASTER'S HOUSE, opposite, were built by M.P.W. Boulton in 1852 for 95 children. The school was enlarged in the 1920s to accommodate children from Little Tew. After the secondary school was built in Chipping Norton in 1928, the children were given a bicycle when they were aged eleven, so that they could ride the six miles to and from school. A scary thought today! There are now about 60 children in the school, which includes a Playgroup.

Leave the village by The Lane and turn left up Butchers Hill.

Beside the road, note two pairs of early nineteenth century cottages, which 'appear to be straight from a pattern book of picturesque designs, with their gabled dormers and lattice windows.'[8]

At the top of the hill, turn left along the Ledwell Road and stop on the left to admire

THE CRICKET GROUND: there has been cricket here at least since the 1920s and probably earlier. The club is renowned for its friendly atmosphere and also for the quality of its ground. The latter is largely due to the devoted work of Gordon Taylor over some fifty years, and he was decorated recently for his services. In September 1938, there was a notable game, when over one hundred members of the Tustian clan gathered from North Oxfordshire, and there were 22 a side. Sixty years later there was a similar gathering, when over one hundred and fifty members of the clan assembled for another remarkable game of cricket.[9]

Continue along the Ledwell Road to the crossroads and turn left down to the Vicarage, where you started your walk.

Notes

1   The Earl of Clarendon, quoted by Richard Ollard, *This War without an Enemy* (1976), 38.

2   The Earl of Clarendon, quoted by Richard Ollard, *This War without an Enemy* (1976), 106.

3   *Victoria County History of Oxford*, xi (Wootton Hundred (Northern Part)), 237.

4   *Victoria County History of Oxford*, xi (Wootton Hundred (Northern Part)), 238.

5   *Banbury Guardian*, 14 October, 1999, Memories of Rev Peter Ettrick.

6   *Banbury Guardian*, 21 October, 1999, Further Memories of Rev Peter Ettrick.

7   *Victoria County History of Oxford,* xi (Wootton Hundred (Northern Part), 243.

8   Sherwood and Pevsner, *The Buildings of England: Oxfordshire* (1974), 628.

9   *Banbury Fayre*, October 1998.

Chapter 9

In the Steps of Flora Thompson

Juniper Hill, Cottisford, and Fringford are all a short distance off the A421 Bicester to Buckingham road. Juniper Hill can either be reached off the Cottisford to Brackley road, still called 'Dicky Brackles' by some, or coming south from Brackley off the A43. It is no longer possible to turn off here if you are coming north on the A43. Although Fringford is some fifteen miles from Banbury, there were regular carriers doing the journey on Thursday market days, at least from the 1820s until the 1930s. This also allowed residents of Juniper Hill and Cottisford to benefit from the services. Indeed, Flora Thompson wrote about Charity Finch, the heroine in *Still the Glides the Stream*, that 'she dearly loved a trip into Banbury in the carrier's cart to see the shops and to enjoy a cup of tea at Bett's.'[1] She also wrote in a letter 'I went there (Banbury) several times in the carrier's cart as a child and had that place partly in mind when creating my Candleford, though most of our relations lived in Buckingham.'[2]

The three villages are now all forever associated with Flora Thompson's *Lark Rise to Candleford*. She was born Flora Timms, in the hamlet of Juniper Hill (Lark Rise) in 1876. In the book she (Laura) recalls her childhood there and walking to school in Cottisford (Fordlow). In 1891, she moved to Fringford (Candleford Green), where she worked in the Post Office until 1896, when she moved to Grayshott in Hampshire. In 1903, she married John Thompson. She wrote poems and short stories for many years but it was not until 1945 that the Lark Rise trilogy was published. The initial 5000 copies were all sold in advance and the book has been in print ever since. Flora died on 21 May 1947 and her ashes were buried in Dartmouth. She shares a gravestone in the shape of an open book with her son, Peter, whose ship had been torpedoed in 1941.

As a local historian and resident of Fringford, I have come to love and appreciate the unique and vivid picture which she gives of village life at the end of the nineteenth century. In many respects, village life had changed very little in the decades before she was born. This was also a

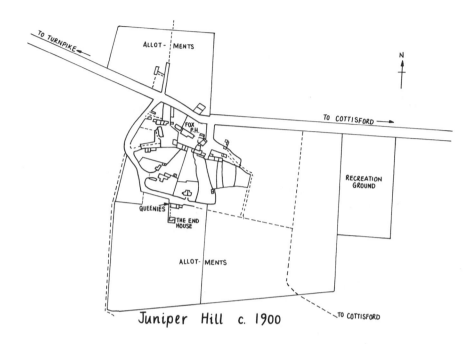

Juniper Hill c. 1900

defining moment just before the agricultural depressions of the 1870s and 1880s and before the impact of major changes in health, housing, and education. There is still much in the three villages to remind us of Flora's time. It therefore seems only appropriate to walk round them in sequence, following in her footsteps. On the ground, while it is possible to combine walks round Juniper Hill and Cottisford, most people would need to drive on to Fringford.

Juniper Hill (Lark Rise)

Juniper Hill has always been part of the parish of Cottisford. In 1754, two cottages were built on 'the Rise', part of the former Cottisford Heath, for the poor.Two more were built soon afterwards, as Cottisford attempted to keep the poor out of their village. After this the hamlet stagnated until the mid-nineteenth century. It was always a poor community, 'the spot God made with the left-overs when he'd finished creating the rest of the earth', and a natural home for squatters.

In 1853, the hamlet suddenly became the focus of attention. There was furious opposition by the 'Juniper Hill Mob' to enclosure of the Common, culminating in the 'Cottisford Riots'. Notices of the proposed enclosure were torn down and surveyors were forced off the Common. Two magis-

Flora Thompson, possibly c.1903 when she married John Thompson (Violet McGovern).

trates and a superintending constable were also driven away and threats were made against any who supported the enclosure. After a summer of discontent, during which warrants of ejection were issued against 42 men, a compromise agreement was signed. This allowed the cottagers to harvest the current year's crops and gave them a 14-year lease on their dwellings at a nominal rent of 5s. per annum. Also, four small free-holders with proof of ownership were allocated plots under the enclosure award.

Enclosure was finally completed in 1856. There were now 20 small owners of land or cottages, of whom 17 had been issued with ejection orders three years before. Most of them were members of the Moss, Savin, and Tuffrey families. By Flora's time in 1881, there were 35 houses including an inn, with a population of 127. This was just over half the total of people living in the parish of Cottisford. Most of the houses had been built on land ceded as 'squatters' rights'. Apparently, there was still widespread belief among the old people that the former Cottisford Heath had been left to the poor and the deeds hidden behind the brass in the village church, 'from whence they were stolen'![3]

We begin our walk outside the old Fox Inn (GR 579325).

In 1999, some 35% of the parish of Cottisford were living in 21 dwellings in Juniper Hill.[4] There has been a marked improvement and enlargement of the houses and many of the old cottages have been demolished. In Flora's day the original houses were in a ring on the Common. Hence the people were used to 'going round the Rise'[5] and it is still possible to do this.

THE FOX INN closed a few years ago but the building remains a
private dwelling and is little changed. It was always The Fox but in
Lark Rise it was called 'The Waggon and Horses' when it was run by
a Catholic landlord, Thomas Harris. There is still a juniper bush in
the front garden to remind us that the hamlet was once covered with
them. Elibut Hulett was the publican between the wars.

Turn right down the track just east of the old inn.

Note the core of old houses on your right as you follow the path to the
allotments. If you turn left at the fence, the path takes you to a stile.
Beyond this, the footpath leads to Cottisford, which would have been
the route sometimes taken by Flora with her younger brother, Edwin
(Edmund). When he started school, she was worried that he might be
bullied if he walked with the other children on the main road. In the
event, he was well able to stand up for himself. He signed up in 1915
and sadly was killed in action later that year.

*We continue our walk to the right round the Rise and pass through a gate
leaving the site of the old allotments on our left.*

OLD SALLY'S HOUSE used to be on the left and it was one of the
largest and most comfortable houses, but it was totally demolished in
Flora's lifetime. Sally and her husband, Dick, were based on Sarah
and Richard Moss.

QUEENIE'S is on the site of the home of Eliza and Thomas Massey
(Queenie and Twister Macey). Eliza was married in 1837 on the day
of Queen Victoria's Coronation and died in Bicester Workhouse.
Like all the women over 50, she took snuff and you would regularly
hear them saying 'Ave a pinch, me dear'.[6] She was noted in Lark Rise
for making lace, which she used to take to Banbury once a year to sell
at the Michaelmas Fair. She was also noted for 'tanging the bees'.
This involved pursuing the swarm when it rose, while tanging an iron
spoon on a coal shovel. She said that this was to ensure that the bees
settled in her garden and that she had a legal right to them.[7]

THE END HOUSE, to which Flora's parents, Albert and Emma,
moved in 1877, is down a short drive behind Queenie's. They had
married in 1875 and rented a cottage in Juniper Hill near Watford

Queenie Massey, the beewoman and lacemaker, in 1880 (Eva Bateman).

Emma Timms, in front on the right, with two of her daughters, Flora on the left, May on the right, c.1900. The lady sitting on the left was another relative. (Violet McGovern).

Tunnel Cottage where Emma Timms's sister, Harriet, and her husband, Thomas were living. Flora was born here in 1876. The cottage was later demolished.

There is a plaque to Flora on The End House but only one original wall remains. The house is detached and looks out over the fields. Both the house and the family were considered slightly superior to others in the hamlet. Albert Timms made more money as a skilled stonemason and he worked away from the community in Brackley for the same firm for thirty-five years.

THE OLD MEETING HOUSE is on the site of Thomas Lavine's cottage, where the 1851 religious census records an evening meeting of thirty. In Flora's time there were still three families of Methodists meeting here on Sunday evenings. Occasionally she attended services, although permission was hard to get as her father did not approve of 'the ranters'. She did not enjoy the services particularly but it made a nice break from boring Sunday evenings at home.

Methodists

Flora's comments on Methodism are interesting. It was 'a poor people's religion, simple and crude; but its adherents brought to it more fervour than was shown by the church congregation, and appeared to obtain more comfort and support from it than the church could give.

Their lives were exemplary.'[8] There seem to have been some doubts about the quality, if not the enthusiasm, of the Methodists in Juniper Hill. They may well have been Primitive Methodists rather than Wesleyans. In June 1877, there is the following comment in the minutes of the Local Preachers meetings: 'It was stated a piece of ground could be had at Juniper for a chapel, enquiry to be made respecting it. The man at whose house services had previously been held had intimated a wish for them to be resumed, but he being of but doubtful character, it was thought best not to have them, unless some other friend would come forward'.[9]

A chapel was never built and occasional visits of inspection by older brethren were recommended. In March 1879, it was reported to the Local Preachers meeting that 'a good congregation had been meeting at a brother's house in Juniper for sometime'. This support clearly continued during Flora's childhood. By contrast, in Cottisford in 1860 the rector could write that 'the greatest unity prevails from almost the absence of dissent'. Such absence of dissent has continued to this day.

THE OLD RACECOURSE: as you move on round the Rise, there is a gap in the hedge on the left. If you look across the field towards the A43, the turnpike in Flora's time, you are looking at the site of the Old Racecourse. The Cottisford Races were still running here in 1827, having been transferred from Northbrook, near Kirtlington. They used to be run at the end of the hunting season.

As you return to the main road, LARKWELL faces you. There was a house here in Flora's time, with more allotments beyond. The house has been completely rebuilt but misleadingly incorporates a smart Victorian letterbox. There was no postal collection from the hamlet in those days and the letterbox was found elsewhere by the present owners.

We have now 'gone round the Rise' and it is time to move on to Cottisford by car or on foot over the stile by the allotments. This is the route which Flora sometimes took to school with her brother, Edwin. If you walk across the fields, you will reach the road out of Cottisford to the A43, which is still called 'Scabgate' by some locals. Turn left and walk to St Mary's Church, which is just round the corner.

Cottisford (Fordlow)

The old village, including the church, the Rectory, and College Farm, lay mainly to the west of the old ford, while the medieval manor was to the east. Eton College owned the manor from 1441 until 1885, when it was sold to Edwards Rousby. To the south of the road there used to be numerous fish-ponds to supply Cottisford House, which was formerly a grange in the hands of the Norman Abbey of Bec. The village pond and the stocks were to the north of the road. Under the Enclosure Award of 1854, the principal beneficiaries were Eton College (489 acres), Sir Henry Dryden and John Kendal (592 acres), and the rector C.S. Harrison.

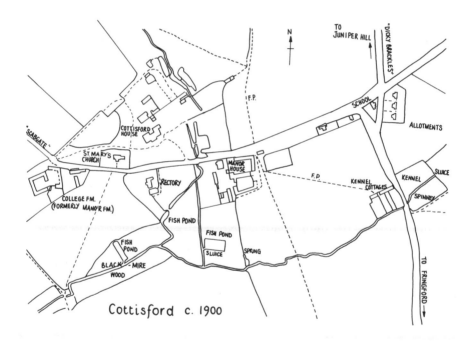

Cottisford c. 1900

In the nineteenth century, the village was dominated by agriculture and the population rose and fell with the fortunes of farming. In 1801, the population was only 106, rising to a peak of 327 in 1871. By 1901 it had fallen to 161, following the agricultural depressions. By 1951 there were only 154 and the present population is about 130. In the late nineteenth century, about half the population were living in Juniper Hill. In Cottisford itself, some 30 to 40 people were living in the group of cottages known as The Warren, which was situated on the north side of

St Mary's Church, Cottisford, south east view in 1825 (J.C. Blomfield).

the village, about half a mile from the crossroads by the School. These had been built in the 1820s, presumably by William Turner to re-house the occupants of the church cottages which he had demolished. The whole place was deserted by 1910 and today there is no trace of it.

We begin our walk at St Mary's Church (GR 587311).

ST MARY'S CHURCH: the churchyard used to be enclosed by cottages
   on three sides. About 1825, William Turner took the lease of
   Cottisford House, altered the roads and demolished the cottages to
   lay out pleasure gardens. On the right of the path to the south
   doorway, there are the remains of an old medieval cross.
13th century: the church and the three-light east window and the south
   porch doorway date from this period, as does the recess on the north
   side of the chancel, with a low stone slab and the stem of a cross.
   The south porch doorway has recently been restored and the old
   sundial replaced.
16th century: on the south wall of the nave, there is a mutilated brass of
   a man in armour with his wife and thirteen children. He may be John
   Samwell who leased the manor from Eton College and died c.1500.

19th century: in the mid-nineteenth century the parishioners were re-seated on the north and south sides of the nave with open sittings; previously the pew seatings were by rank. Charles Harrison (1853-96) was the first resident rector. There is a plaque to him in the chancel and a photograph in the vestry. As Mr Ellison in Lark Rise, he was particularly remembered for a sermon after a Liberal victory in the General Election of 1886 in which he denounced liberalism as ' a bloody cause'.[10]

By 1860, the church was 'very dilapidated' and a thorough restoration was undertaken. The square-headed windows were 'gothicised', the small belfry was taken down, and a new font and altar were installed. Bishop Wilberforce preached at the re-opening in 1861. In 1867, the living of Cottisford was combined with that of Hardwick-with-Tusmore, about a mile to the south-west.

20th century: in 1935, the Revd Dr Sherard Statham (rector 1912-47) purchased the seventeenth-century screen, which now forms the present vestry. Originally it was installed across the chancel in memory of his wife but it was moved in 1969. The eighteenth-century organ, which came from the chapel in Steane Park near Brackley, was presented to the church in memory of Dr Statham. The donor was Ethel Fletcher, who had looked after his household throughout his years in Cottisford. The fine eighteenth-century Royal Coat of Arms remains in its original position, high above the aisle. A plaque to Flora Thompson has been placed on the north wall of the nave.

COLLEGE FARM, formerly Manor Farm, was built in the eighteenth century and has been recently refurbished. On the west side by the track to Hardwick and Tusmore, some of the outbuildings have been converted to private dwellings. In the late nineteenth century, Tusmore was owned by the Earls of Effingham and the locals took a pride in 'our Earl'. When the flag could be seen flying on his mansion, they would say 'I see our family's at home again'.[11] The 2nd Earl had bought the estate in 1857 and significantly enlarged the house. In the 1870s, when Flora was born, some 20 staff were employed there and many more local people would have been working on the estate.

In 1960, Lord Bicester built a new house but this was pulled down recently by Wafic Said to make way for another new house. 'The new Tusmore Park is, in scale and quality, the finest Classical country

Tusmore Park, the new house, 2005 (Wafic Said and June Buck / Country Life Picture Library).

house built in Britain since the Second World War, and perhaps the grandest since Manderston in Berwickshire, in the Edwardian age.'[12]

THE RECTORY: there was a rectory on this site in the seventeenth century, and a datestone at the back shows 1618 or 1619. The tithe barn also has a datestone of 1651, probably the date of its restoration. The present rectory was built in 1821 but it was significantly enlarged by Charles Harrison soon after he arrived in 1853. Note the brick extensions to the rear.

COTTISFORD HOUSE: there was a grange here by 1306, in the hands of the Norman Abbey of Bec. It was administered by the Prior of Ogbourne, who had a bailiff in Cottisford. There was a granary, garden, dovecote, and fishery attached. In 1441, the manor passed to Eton College, who let it to a series of lesser gentry: Samwells, Ardens, and Pettys. Robert Petty was the grandfather of Anthony Wood, the seventeenth-century Oxfordshire historian.

By 1606 at the latest, the College had built a new mansion for its tenants. About 1700 Laurence Lord built another new house. This was leased for a time to James Eyre, Chief Justice of the Common Pleas, and in 1773 to John Russell Greenhill, rector of Fringford, who paid the princely sum of £7,300 for the lease. In 1825, William

Turner took the lease and made extensive alterations and additions. It was he who demolished the cottages round the church and laid out pleasure gardens. In 1842, James Rousby leased it and in 1885 his son, Edwards Rousby, bought it from the College.

In *Lark Rise*, Laura recalls the day of the school treat at the Manor House. The previous teacher, Miss Holmes, had always had her tea with the children. Miss Shepherd was more ambitious and decided to go to the front door. 'She had the satisfaction of ringing the front-door bell and drinking tea in the drawing-room; but it was a short-lived triumph. In a very few minutes she was out in the servants' hall, passing bread and butter to her charges and whispering to one of her monitors that "Dear Mrs Bracewell gave me my tea first, because, as she said, she knew that I was anxious to get back to my children".'[13]

In 1929, there was a serious fire resulting in large-scale rebuilding. In the last few years, the house, outbuildings, and garden have been beautifully restored. The fine old dovecote remains, possibly restored in the sixteenth century judging by the old bricks.

Walk across the brook, site of the old ford, and look to your right.

MANOR FARM was built in the fourteenth century and is one of the oldest dwellings in Oxfordshire. It was remodelled in the sixteenth and seventeenth centuries, when a south wing was added. There is a sixteenth-century parlour on the west side. The original house consisted of a north-south block, with two small projections on the west. The main block had a hall and solar on the first floor. A number of old windows survive. In 1857, the 2nd Earl of Effingham bought it from the Ramsays and leased it to tenant farmers. Joseph Waters, the farmer whom Flora knew, lived here for nine years before moving in 1891 to Home Farm, Shelswell.

THE OLD SCHOOL, at the crossroads, was built in 1857 by Charles Harrison, with a small grant from the 'National Society for Promoting the Education of the Poor in the Principles of the Established Church'. In the following year he built a teacher's residence, attached to the schoolroom. Flora walked daily to Fordlow School, where she was taught by Miss Holmyard (Miss Holmes), who married the squire's gardener. She has much to say in Lark Rise about the school and her schooling in the 1880s.

By 1903, the school was 'in every way inadequate' and the teacher's house fit to be condemned. In 1904, sweeping changes were made, resulting in two separate schoolrooms being provided, one for infants and one for older children. The teacher's cottage was probably removed at the same time. In 1929, the school was reorganised as a junior school and the senior pupils were transferred to Fringford. The school was finally closed in 1968 and the pupils transferred to Finmere. Sadly, subsequent conversion to a private dwelling, with numerous alterations and extensions, has removed almost all the features of the old school building.

THE NEW COTTAGES, across from the school, now known as Nos.1 to 6 Hethe Road, were built by the 3rd Earl of Effingham in 1869 for 'the shepherd, the blacksmith, and other superior farm-workers.'[14] There are datestones on some of them, as there are on some similar cottages in neighbouring Hardwick, which were built at the same time.

You can now retrace your steps towards the church. If you wish to return to Juniper Hill, take the footpath on the right opposite Manor Grange. If you wish to walk some 2 miles to Fringford, take the footpath on the left by Mill Stone Barn via Hethe to Fringford Bridge. Cross the bridge and take the footpath on the left across the field to Rectory Lane and turn right to The Green.

For a more scenic route to Fringford, take the footpath on the left below the New Cottages. Walk past the lake, turn right at the stile and follow the footpath across Shelswell Park to the site of the old Shelswell Manor (pulled down in the 1980s). Branch right by the old stable block (now converted), cross the fields to Willaston and on to Fringford Bridge.

Fringford (Candleford Green)

Fringford is an ancient site and seems to have been inhabited for most, if not all, of the past two thousand years. The village lies on sloping ground in a loop of a tributary of the River Ouse. The name is thought to mean 'ford of the people of Fera', a Saxon tribe or family group, who were here well before the Norman Conquest. There were still traces of a ford in the late nineteenth century. There are traces of an earlier Romano-British settlement from the late second century to the fourth century, in Crosslands, situated in the centre of the village. There is also evidence of a possible Romano-British villa at Fringford Lodge on the right of the road to Bicester. Recent excavations in Farriers Close revealed evidence of Saxon and medieval settlements.[15] Significant medieval remains have also been found at Fringford Manor.

In the seventeenth century, there were some 30 houses and a population of about 130. By the time of the Enclosure Award in 1762, some 400 to 500 acres had already been enclosed by agreement, most of it for the manor owned by Sir Fulke Greville. The principal beneficiaries of the Award were Greville (385 acres), the Revd John Russell Greenhill (227 acres), Anthony Addington of Hall Farm (89 acres), and Eton College (71 acres). As we have seen, Eton College also owned most of the neighbouring village of Cottisford. Unlike many other villages in the area, Fringford had no manor house after the sixteenth century. In the eighteenth and nineteenth centuries the village was dominated by the Trotman and Harrison families, the squires of Shelswell Manor. In 1844, it was reported that 'Nearly if not the whole of Fringford is the property of JHS Harrison Esq.'[16] Shelswell Manor was abandoned in the 1960s and finally pulled down in the 1980s.

In the nineteenth century, the village was also dominated by a series of well-connected, wealthy rectors, who were prepared to make substantial contributions to the church and parish. Late nineteenth-century Fringford is forever associated with Flora Thompson, who worked in the village Post Office from 1891 to 1897 after she had left school in Cottisford. In *Lark Rise* she largely bases Candleford Green on her memories of Fringford in those years. By 1801, there were some 50 houses and a population of 252. As with other villages in the area, the population was largely dependent on agriculture. It reached its peak of 479 in 1871, but by 1901 had fallen to 335. In 1951, there were still only 331 inhabitants.

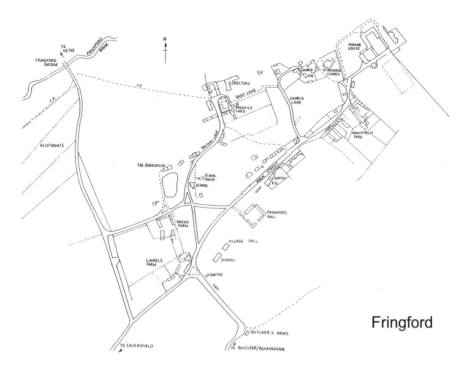

Fringford

The 1852 trade directory records 7 farmers and 12 trades and up to 1939
this level remained more or less the same. Carrier links with Banbury
began in 1829 with Patrick Butler going to The Flying Horse on
Thursdays. After 1870 the main links were with The George in
Cowfair, with James and William Grantham operating from then
until the 1920s. After that the Banbury connection was by omnibus.
Other recurring names include the Gibbards, who farmed at Laurels
Farm c.1860 to 1939, the Prices, who were painters, decorators, and
plumbers from the 1860s until after the Second World War, and the
Plumbs, who were blacksmiths from the 1890s until the 1940s.
Since the War, following a number of housing developments, the popu-
lation has nearly doubled to about 600. Initial housing developments
in the 1960s, in Church Close and St Michael's Close, were followed
by those in Manor Road and later ones in Crosslands and Farriers
Close. The village still has a primary school and a pub but no shops.

We begin our walk at the Butchers Arms by the Cricket Ground (GR 605286).

The BUTCHERS ARMS is seventeenth- and eighteenth-century and it
was definitely licensed by 1735. In 1774, there was a Bricklayers

Arms in the village – possibly the same inn. Albert Green ran the pub
from 1913 to 1955, and he also ran a taxi service. The pub which is
said to be haunted by the ghost of 'Rose Brennan' who may have
been murdered here, continues to flourish, providing a warm
welcome and fine food.

The MALT HOUSE, behind the pub, dates from the eighteenth century
or earlier. A doorway in the back room of the pub used to lead
through to the Malt House. There used to be a smithy up Green
Lane, the path on the north side.

The COUNCIL HOUSES in Wise Crescent opposite and on the
Stratton Audley Road beyond the pub, were built in the early 1950s.
They had all the modern conveniences, which represented a major
advance in the standard of housing in the village. Initially, weekly
rents for the two-bedroomed type were 15s. inclusive of rates. By
1958 rents were 18s.,with rates an extra 4s.11d. plus 1s.3d. for an
electric cooker. In the 1990s all the houses in the Stratton Audley
Road were modernised and refaced.

*Walk back past the cricket ground to the large chestnut tree. About 50 yards from
the pub, where there is a slight hollow by the path, there used to be a small pond
on which the children would skate in the winter.*

The CRICKET GROUND was presented to the village by Henry
Chinnery. The Cricket Club celebrated its centenary in 2001,
although in Candleford Green in the 1890s the rector, Mr Delafield,
is said to have put cricket 'upon a proper footing, with an eleven of
young men and practice nights for boys'.[17] Interestingly, there is a
photograph of a women's eleven in 1915!

SUNNYSIDE COTTAGE used to be the home of Phyllis and Arthur
Omar after the Second World War. Phyllis, whose sister Ivy ran the
pub in neighbouring Hethe, had a shop here for many years. It
continued as a shop until the late 1970s. The house was rebuilt in the
1980s.

SUNNYSIDE HOUSE, next door, was the site of a smithy, where
Albert Jackman worked until his death in 1951. Ernest Perrin bought
it in 1953 when he left the Old Forge, and he ran it with his brother
until it closed in the 1960s.

LAURELS FARM, on the corner by the chestnut tree, dates from the
late seventeenth or early eighteenth century but parts may be even

Laurels Farm crossroads, looking towards the Butchers Arms, with the old farrier's workshop in the foreground, 1930s (OCC).

earlier. Some cellars and an old staircase survive. The Gibbard family were farming here from the 1850s until the outbreak of the Second World War, when the Wise family bought the farm. There used to be an off-licence here and people remember sitting outside with their drinks. During the War they used to drink in the air-raid shelter, which had been dug in the garden. The new houses in The Laurels, behind the farmhouse, were built when the farmland was sold in the 1980s.

Turn right to admire the classic Village Green.

The Green
The classic setting of a medieval village grouped round the Green survives. The old farmhouses, Laurels Farm and Green Farm on the left and Hall Farm beyond the village hall, all date from well before the Enclosure Award of 1762. In the sixteenth century there was also a manor on the far side of the Green, on the site of the Old School. After Enclosure, new farms like Waterloo Farm and Glebe Farm were built outside the village. Waterloo Farm, on the back road to

Caversfield, was built by Squire Harrison in 1815 soon after his purchase of the Shelswell Estate, and he 'named it after the great victory, which was at that time the talk of every tongue.'[18]

The CHURCH OF ENGLAND PRIMARY SCHOOL, on the right, was opened in 1973 to replace the Old National School on the other side of the Green. There are about 100 children in the school now. In February 2003, the Playgroup also moved across the Green into a new building on the school site. The new Playgroup site used to be known as 'Jackman's Garden', after Albert Jackman of Sunnyside. Early in the 1900s there was an old cottage here, with two large willow trees in the garden.

The VILLAGE HALL was built by Henry Chinnery on land given by the local squire, Edward Slater-Harrison. It was formally opened by Mr Chinnery in June 1900 and presented to the village as a reading-room for the men of the village and a place for meetings and entertainments. In 1901, it was described in the local press as 'the new parish room', where tea and entertainment were provided on New Year's Day. The entertainment included singing, recitations, and a cinematograph exhibition by Mr Timms of Oxford.[19]

Walk across the Green past Laurels Farm.

GREEN FARM is late seventeenth-century, with some eighteenth-century and more recent additions. Parts, including an old floor, may be even earlier. The two-storey building on the right is a separate dwelling, which has been refurbished. The eighteenth-century barn to the rear has recently been converted to a private dwelling.

CROW LANE was the old name for the lane leading to the Hethe road, as there used to be elm trees on both sides full of crows. There were gardens on the west side, some of them used by the children from the Old School for growing vegetables.

ALLOTMENTS: known as The 'Bridge Ground' allotments, these used to be on the left of the Hethe road before Fringford Bridge. An 1899 plan of these allotments, with a schedule of allotment rentals, survives. There were 65 allotments of varying sizes, with rentals from 2s.1d. to 5s.3d. per half-year, payable on Lady Day and Michaelmas. There were also some allotments known as 'Crabdy (or Crabtree) Piece' on the right of the back road near Waterloo Farm. They were all given up in the 1950s.

The Old Bakehouse and the village pond c.1950, before the fence was erected round it (Bill Plumb).

THE COTTAGE, on the corner of Crow Lane, was sold by John
    Dewar-Harrison 'for a song and a handshake' (as were a number of
    other properties in the village) to Roy and Myrtle Ayris in the late
    1950s. It was a seventeenth- or eighteenth-century thatched cottage,
    which Roy, with much local help, rebuilt almost completely.

The OLD BAKEHOUSE dates from the seventeenth century. Harold
    Crook was the baker between the Wars. He used to wear a cape and a
    big black hat which scared the children! In those days the baker
    would still roast Sunday joints for the villagers for 2d. or 3d. Les
    Morgan was the last man to run the bakery in the 1960s and he is still
    remembered for the quality of his cakes! The pond used to be the
    village pond but the Shelswell Estate sold it to a previous owner of
    the house who erected the original fence round it. Mr Rawlinson
    cleaned up the pond in 1976 and erected a new fence.

*There is a public footpath to the left of the house, which leads to Bull Field and
Fringford Bridge. From there you can walk across the fields to Hethe and
Cottisford.*

The OLD SCHOOL was built as a National (i.e. Church of England)
    School in 1866 by the rector, Henry de Salis, on land leased from
    John Dewar-Harrison. This was the site of the sixteenth-century

The Old School in the 1950s before the building was joined to the Hut. The Hut was demolished as part of the recent conversion to a private house (Judy Legg).

North Manor occupied by the Wenmans, and later of the parish Poor House, known as 'The Barracks' (pulled down c.1830). The South Manor was probably on the site of Moat Farm (formerly Cotmore Farm), down the back road to Caversfield.

The Old School was church-aided until 1951 when it was handed over to the Local Education Authority. In 1940, pupil numbers had risen to 160 with the arrival of some 50 evacuees. By 1949, however, they were down to 69 and the problems of a small school had become too serious for the managers. After the school transferred to the new site in 1973, the building was used as a Victorian Study Centre. The site was sold in 2004 and the school building converted to a superior private house. Conversion included the demolition of the wooden hut extension, which had been used by the Shelswell Playgroup since the 1980s. Demolition was not before time, as the hut had been erected in 1931 as an extra classroom at a cost of £125! The Playgroup relocated to a new building on the school site in 2003.

The OLD SCHOOL HOUSE was built in 1876 on land leased from
Lord Sidmouth, the owner of Hall Farm. Edwin Blackburn and his
wife, who were the first teachers in the National School, were the first
occupants. The headmasters lived here until 1964.

COTTAGES ON THE GREEN: Nos.1 and 2 were built about 1960,
Nos.3 and 4 about 1950, and Nos.5 and 6 in 1929. Albert White used
to live in No.6. He always smoked a pipe, grew his own tobacco and
hung it out in the attic – the smell is still remembered!

For many years Albert Price lived in Rose Cottage, an old thatched
cottage on the site of No.1. Albert, known as 'Noah', was a
legendary character in the village. He was a painter/decorator like
others in the Price family. He rode an old motor bike with a sidecar in
which he kept his ladder and all his decorating equipment. It was
only on rare occasions that this equipment seems to have been used.
He was a great talker and, as one builder used to say, 'Lock him in
and keep him in'! Otherwise no work was done. When he was
commissioned by Albert Green to redecorate the pub, he painted one
room and then left without returning!

SPRING HOUSE was built very recently on part of the garden of No.6,
where there used to be a pump for use by those living on the Green.

HALL FARM, formerly Fringford Hall, dates from the early seventeenth century with eighteenth- and twentieth-century alterations.
Part of the north end may date from the fourteenth century. The two-
storey addition on the south-west side was built in the late
seventeenth century. A brick dovecote survives at the rear between
the ground and first floors. The Addington family have owned the
farm for some four hundred years, although the family have not lived
here since 1746. Dr Anthony Addington was doctor to William Pitt
'The Elder' (the first Earl of Chatham) and to George III during his
'madness'. In 1788, he was the only doctor successfully to predict the
king's recovery from what is now known to have been porphyria. His
son, Henry, became Speaker and Prime Minister (1801-4) and the
first Lord Sidmouth. He is also remembered as the minister who
introduced Income Tax!

Main Street

The OLD FORGE, on the right, dates from the mid-eighteenth century
with twentieth-century alterations. It used to be the sub-post office
where Flora Thompson worked as assistant postmistress from 1891

The Old Forge c.1898 with Frederick Plumb in the cart. The smartly dressed boys were two of Kesia Whitton's nephews on a visit from Liverpool (Bill Plumb).

to 1897. In Flora's time the forge and the Post Office were both run by Kesia Whitton (Dorcas Lane). Kesia's husband, John, died shortly after Flora's arrival. Both of them were very large; John weighed over 22 stone and Kesia over 18 stone! When she died in 1898, Frederick Plumb, who was one of the blacksmiths, had to take out the left-hand upstairs bedroom window so that her coffin could be lowered down a ladder. It was too big to carry down the stairs! You can still see where he subsequently patched up the window. The Whittons' maid, Zilpha Hinks (Zillah), died in 1900 and her grave, marked by a cast-iron cross, is in the churchyard near the front gate.

After Kesia Whitton's death, Frederick Plumb took over the tenancy and the Plumb family continued to live there until the 1990s, although the forge closed in 1953. The Automobile Association sign on the front of the house was originally put up c.1926. It was common at the time to put these signs up on village forges. Along with all signposts, it was taken down during the Second World War but Bill Plumb found it in a shed after the War and put it back up.

MIDWAY was built by Bill Plumb in the early 1970s in the orchard of The Old Forge, where his father, William, was still living.

William Plumb (in smock) with Thomas Deeley in the garden of the Old Forge. Note the privy in the background (Bill Plumb).

ROSEMARY COTTAGE was built in 1952 on the site of an old thatched cottage. Jimmy Gerring, who was the sexton for many years, used to live here.

GANDERS is on the site of a thatched cottage where the Granthams lived at one time. William Grantham was a carrier, like his father James, and later a coal merchant until he retired in 1936. He kept his cart and, later, his coal lorry in a barn on the corner of Church Lane. The Granthams have had the longest family connection with the village, stretching back some 400 years, and William's son, Bill, has only recently left the village. In 1847, James Grantham was keeping the Butchers Arms and he was also a baker. His son, James, became a carrier in 1874, going to The George in Banbury every Thursday, and also to Bicester, Brackley, and Buckingham every week.

Bill likes to imagine the hard times which his family and many others must have had during the agricultural depressions in the nineteenth century. In May 1884, for example, the local newspaper recorded that James's wife, Sarah, was in court for stealing butter in Bicester. The chairman, W.W.M.Dewar, took a lenient view of the offence and she was given 21 days hard labour in Oxford! Apparently, he could have given her three months in prison with hard labour!

ROSECROFT is the only eighteenth-century cottage to survive on the left side of Main Street. Cecil and Agnes Cross used to live here. Cecil was the butcher and his slaughter house was next door on the corner of what is now Crosslands. Agnes was the church organist for many years. There used to be a small cottage on the other side of Rosecroft.

GABLE COTTAGE, on the right, was originally two eighteenth-century cottages. An 1818 datestone on the rear part may be the date of some later alterations. Note that the gable-end fronts onto Main Street. This was common where there was limited frontage available on the main street and a cottage had to be squeezed into a very narrow space. It is also interesting to note on the gable-end the steep pitch of the original thatched roof.

STONE GAP COTTAGE is part of a line of four cottages, along with The Cottage, Fox Cottage (formerly Amberley), and Bakery Cottage. They all date from the mid-eighteenth century or earlier. The porches were added in the twentieth century. Recently, the stonework of Fox Cottage and The Cottage has been finely restored in authentic fashion. Stone Gap Cottage was the old sweet and cigarette shop run by Lizzie Grantham, Bill's aunt, from the 1930s until she retired in the late 1950s. Bill recalls that she used to put her hand on the scales to make sure that she never gave the children too many sweets! James Grantham, the carrier, lived in Amberley. On the left of the house is the old cart entrance with wide plank doors.

FRINGFORD COTTAGE was built in 1938 by Miss Joyce Tomkinson. She was a great character and played a leading part in village life, as Chair of the Parish Council, Chair of Managers of the School, and President of the Cricket Club. During the Second World War she ran the hospital/recovery home at Tusmore. She was greatly loved and a little feared by the village! She rode side-saddle to hounds until her early 70s and never missed a meet until a few months before her death.

FOLLY FIELDS was the site of Folly Barn, which belonged to the Sumners at Church Farm until after the Second World War. The

Main Street in the 1920s before the porches were added to the thatched cottages (Gordon Allen).

Buckingham family bought the barn then and built the house here.

FOLLY COTTAGES date from the eighteenth century. The two present
cottages were once a line of three smaller thatched cottages and you
can see where some of the old doorways have been filled in. The
porches were added in the twentieth century.

Evacuees lived in No.1 during the Second World War. Mr and Mrs
Dudley and their family lived in No.3. He was a butcher in Twyford,
Bucks and used to walk the five miles there and back each day to
work! Nos.2 and 3 have romance attached to them, as they were
made into one after Chris Singleton (No.3) married Jane (No.2) in
the late 1970s. This caused some confusion for the milkman among
others!

BEAGLE COTTAGE and LILAC COTTAGE both date from the early
eighteenth century. There used to be three cottages here and you can
see where some of the old doorways have been blocked up. Inside
there are still three old winder staircases. The cottages have been
renovated and rethatched recently.

HOLLY COTTAGE, opposite, formerly Stonehaven, was built on the
site of a thatched cottage. Bill and Hannah Grantham lived here in
the 1940s for a rent of 3s. per week and had no electricity until 1948!

ST MICHAEL'S CLOSE was developed in the late 1960s on the site of
the old Mansfield Yard. There used to be a group of old cottages in

Elizabeth Hinks, with her lace pillow and bobbins, like Queenie in Lark Rise. She is sitting with William 'Joe' Spacey in front of his cottage in Mansfield Yard, late 1920s (Gladys Hinks).

the Yard, all of which were demolished, except Yew Tree Cottage. The Yard was commonly known as "Birdie Cage" after Margaret Bird, who owned most of the cottages. William Elderfield, who had a thriving clock and watch repair business, lived in one of the cottages and had a separate workshop in the Yard. He used to do repairs for Harrods in London in addition to all his local work. Older residents recall the hundreds of pounds' worth of clocks and watches ticking away in his workshop. William was a blacksmith when he joined the army during the First World War. His delicate touch was discovered then and he was trained as a watchmaker.

DAIRY COTTAGE was built very recently on a small plot which had been marked out for a house early in the last century. There was a dairy here when the Sumners of Church Farm House were supplying the village with milk.

YEW TREE COTTAGE, in Mansfield Yard, was built by David Mansfield in the late nineteenth century and his name is still carved above the fireplace. Ernest and Emily Hinks used to live here with their daughter, Gladys, as did her grandparents before them. Emily, and later Gladys, ran a small shop. The cottage has since been enlarged. Gladys still lives in St Michael's Close. She recalls that her father, who was a carpenter by trade, also kept pigs and hens in a paddock leased from John Dewar-Harrison next to the Yard. After the First World War, when it was very difficult to find employment, Ernest used to 'get on his bike' and cycle to Coventry to look for work. During the Second World War he was a ganger employed by the RAF to do all sorts of 'rural jobs' on the Shelswell airfield.

The VILLAGE PUMP, opposite Mansfield Yard, was for use by this end of the village until the arrival of mains water c.1960. It was thought that the pump water was infected by the trees, so people continued to use water from the wells for drinking. There were a great number of wells in the village, including no less than three at the Old Forge. The thatched cover was put over the pump in memory of Douglas Crowther, who died in 1987.

THE LODGE was built in the Gothic style by Mr Chinnery in 1898, when he was rebuilding Fringford Manor. Jim Wyatt lived here with his family when he took over the tenancy of Manor Farm just before the Second World War. His grandson lives here now. Just beyond the Lodge there used to be two sets of gates at the entrances to the Manor.

FRINGFORD MANOR was converted from a farmhouse in 1899 to 1900 by Henry Chinnery, who leased the property from John Dewar-Harrison. In 1948, Dewar-Harrison wanted to build new houses for some of his workers. When he found that this was impossible because of shortages after the War, he converted the Manor into six houses for them. There were more conversions in the 1980s, to the west barns, where the Manor's milking parlour had been, and in the stable yard. In No.6 Laura Powell ran the Post Office (said to be the smallest one in England) from 1949 to 1986.

During the Second World War a convent junior school was evacuated to the Manor. The senior school was evacuated to Swift's House, Stoke Lyne. Norah Morgan recalls how both schools used to walk in crocodile every Sunday to the Catholic Church in Hethe, the juniors in dark brown uniforms, the seniors in dark blue ones.

MANOR FARM was built by John Wyatt in the 1980s on the site of the Manor's kitchen garden and orchard. His father had inherited the farm and adjoining land from John Dewar-Harrison in 1967. There is now a herb farm here. The houses in Manor Road were also built on the site of the old orchard in the 1980s.

Walk down to the end of the road and look into the private courtyard.

The coachman and other staff of the Chinnerys lived here. The grooms' messroom and the tack room (Coach House Cottage) were on the right next to the carriage rooms (Coach House). Straight ahead is Gardener's Cottage. The converted Old Stables are on the left.

Walk back to the churchyard.

The CHURCHYARD was enlarged in 1875 and 1906 by gifts of land from Eton College and the Harrison family. The War Memorial on the left records the names of the seven men who gave their lives in the two World Wars. The unusual cast-iron crosses, which you can see over a number of the graves, date from 1888 to 1937. There are more crosses of this type in Fringford (24) than anywhere else in Oxfordshire and five of them were made at Stratford-on-Avon by John Smith. These cast-iron crosses were available nationally in various forms and they were very popular because they were much cheaper than stone memorials.

ST MICHAEL'S AND ALL ANGELS CHURCH stands on the site of an early wooden building, which may have served the Saxon villagers for hundreds of years. The earliest part of the present stone church dates from the early twelfth century, when Baron Manessah Arsic built a new church and granted it to the priory of Black Monks, instituted by his father at Cogges, near Witney. The south door, although much restored, dates from this period, as do the two northern arches of the nave.

13th century: on the south side of the nave, there are some men's heads carved on one pillar making faces at some grotesque women's heads on the opposite pillar. These seem to be a thirteenth-century carver's joke!

16th century: the roughly carved rood-screen dates from this period.

18th century: there are two memorials to the Addington family of Hall Farm on the wall of the north aisle.

19th century: the church was largely rebuilt in this period. From 1814 to

1894 Fringford was fortunate to enjoy the considerable personal wealth, intellectual ability and social standing of three 'regal rectors': Henry Roundell, Henry de Salis and Cadwallader Coker. All three are commemorated in the church.

In 1821, a new chancel was built and in 1829 the north aisle was repaired. In 1831, the present stone tower was constructed to replace the wooden belfry. In 1842, the pulpit was installed, using seventeenth-century panels from neighbouring Hardwick Manor, and the vestry was built. In 1857, the south aisle was enlarged under the guidance of the diocesan architect, G.E.Street. There are two fonts in the south aisle, an octagonal one possibly from the sixteenth-century, presented by Henry Roundell, and a round one of 1880 in memory of Anne King, who lived at Waterloo Farm.

20th century: in the early 1900s Henry Chinnery paid for the north chapel to be rebuilt. Two clerestory windows were added, the ceiling was re-decorated, and stained glass was placed in the east window. The angel wall-painting was painted in 1902 and restoration in 2004 revealed that the artist's name was T.F.M.Sheard, who lived in the Vale of the White Horse and exhibited fourteen works at the Royal Academy between 1891 and 1903. The fine altar in the north aisle was given by Mrs Marjorie Chinnery in 1972. Some local people still refer to the north aisle as the 'Chinnery Chapel'.

The carvings: in 1839, John Rogers, the organist and village carpenter, carved new seats for the nave. He also made the fine casing for the organ, which was given by Henry de Salis in 1853. The beautiful carving on the pew-ends was done after the First World War by Charlie Freeman, who lived on the Green. He had been severely disabled by frostbite in Canada and did much of his work lying down in the aisles. He also carved the vestry wall and the choir-stalls.

The stained glass: there was so much stained glass installed in the nineteenth century that, as a later rector said, 'no one can now read his prayer book without electric light'! The Roundell family filled all the windows in the chancel. In the north aisle, one window is dedicated to Cadwallader Coker and his family and another one to John Dewar, who was killed in the Boer War in 1900.

The bells: one of the bells was cast by R.Atton of Buckingham in 1617 and two of them by R.Chandler in 1702. The small Sanctus bell was cast c.1800 by Robert Wills of Aldbourne, Wiltshire. Unfortunately, because of the present dilapidated state of the tower, a proper ringing of the bells is not possible.

There have been few alterations to the church in the last hundred years. Not surprisingly, restoration is now much needed and £50,000 is being raised for this purpose. The church is one of ten in the Shelswell Group of Churches in the Diocese of Oxford, which are now combined under one rector.

Leave the churchyard by the small gate at the north-west corner and enter Church Lane.

As you leave, note the memorial on the right to the Revd Coker and members of his family, including his son, Lewis, who died at Ekowe in 1879, aged 19. He was serving as a midshipman in the Naval Brigade on HMS Active during the Anglo-Zulu Wars. Many of the Coker family are commemorated in St Edburg's Church in Bicester.

Church Lane

As a result of the changes in occupancy over the last 150 years, the lane has been variously called Judds Lane, Sumners Lane and now Church Lane.

CHURCH FARM HOUSE, formerly Eton College Farm, was probably a timber-framed farmhouse of the sixteenth century and there may well have been earlier farm buildings on the site which belonged to Eton College. By the late nineteenth century the farmhouse had been converted into cottages. The Judd family, who were mostly agricultural labourers and coal hauliers, lived here as tenants from c.1860 to 1921. In 1921, the College sold the farm to Harold Judd, when they were selling all their remaining property in Fringford and Cottisford.

The Judd family had a long connection with the village from at least the early nineteenth century. Thomas Judd was the parish clerk for thirty-seven years from the late 1860s for the princely annual fee of £5, also supplying coal, gravel, wood and straw, sweeping the flues and ringing the bells. He used to collect coal from Finmere station and store it in bunkers in the farmyard. The remains of the bunkers and some lumps of coal were found in 1990 when some of the stables were removed.

From 1928 to 1965 the Sumners farmed here and ran a dairy. During much of this period the house was divided into three cottages. By 1965 the property was in a very poor state of repair. Fortunately, in the late 1960s the house was restored and made into one dwelling again. The remains of the old granary were pulled down in the late 1980s, when an annexe for grooms was built on the south end. The annexe has now been incorporated into the main house, the old stables have been largely rebuilt and the old cowshed restored.

ROSEMARY COTTAGE opposite is a late Victorian cottage built by the rector, Cadwallader Coker. George 'Snobby' Judd, a shoemaker and an older brother of Reuben at Church Farm House, lived here until his death in 1935.

FORGE MILL HOUSE was built in at the beginning of the 1990s by Paddy McMahon, the Irish showjumper, after he sold Church Farm House. It was named after his famous horse, Penward Forge Mill.

CHURCH COTTAGES, Nos.1 and 2, are late Victorian cottages, built by the Revd Coker. No.2 has been extended recently.

Take the small footpath on the right after Church Cottages.

GHOST ALLEY is an apt name for what was once a rather spooky path. Is there a ghost from the Civil War skirmish near Fringford in March 1645 when the Royalists were retreating from Finmere? The explanation is probably more mundane. This was the hand-bier route for 'walking funerals' from the undertaker, Billy Judd on Rectory Lane.

Notice the long garden on the left. It was here that all the cottages in Prentice Yard used to have their gardens and hovels (i.e. toilets) over on the far side. On the right is the long boundary wall of the Old Rectory garden.

The OLD RECTORY in 1756 was a mere thatched cottage, too small for the rector's family. The Revd Roundell (1814-52) enlarged it considerably between 1817 and 1818 at a cost of £2,098, and made further additions later. These alterations included the larger rooms on the east side and the refacing of the whole house with local stone. The kitchen and laundry were in the earlier west wing of the house, next to the stables and coach-house. There is now a separate occu-pant in part of the west wing. Note the old bell on the roof, which may have been used to call the children to their lessons when there was a school in the barn next door.

The drive to the Rectory used to go round the back of Bancroft, which was an orchard, and up to the old front of the house. Traces of the old front door and doorstep can still be seen, where there is a curve in the stonework. A cart-track used to cross Bull Field (formerly Bancroft) and connect the Rectory to the Hethe road. The large garden and the broad view over towards Willaston are to be admired. There are also some fine trees, planted by Roundell and his successors, and a substantial walled garden.

BANCROFT was built for the Standens in 1964 when Jack Standen retired as headmaster of the Old School and moved out of the Old School House. The old barn on the right, together with the Bancroft property, used to be owned by the Church, and there used to be other old outbuildings on the property. In 1853, the Revd de Salis noted 'No school room. Half of the Old Tithe Barn fitted up by me as a School House for which purpose it now answers very well'. There were 35 children here and 20 at an infant school until the National School was built in 1866.

RECTORY LANE, formerly known simply as 'The Other Street', is a very old road, which was probably used by drovers in Saxon times. They used to take their sheep to Brackley, which was a thriving wool centre. The old lane went round to the left of the Bancroft property and continued across the field down to 'Fera's Ford' and up to Willaston. There were still traces of a stone-paved way to Willaston in the nineteenth century. The young Flora Timms would have taken this route from the Post Office up to Shelswell Manor in the 1890s.

FRINGFORD HOUSE, formerly Rectory Cottage or The Cottage, used to be on glebe land owned by the rector. It seems to have been rented out to various tenants until Ellis and Katharine Chinnery bought it in 1921, when they changed the name. The small central core of the house dates from the seventeenth century. The south wing was added in the late nineteenth century. Extensions on the north end, the west side, and a further one on the south side, were added by the Chinnerys between 1921 and 1922.

CANDLEFORD MEWS includes the Pump House and the Coach House, which used to be stables and outbuildings for Fringford House. When Katharine Chinnery died in 1978, they were converted and Candleford Cottage was built at the end of the Mews.

MEADOW VIEW, opposite the Rectory gates, was part of a row of five cottages built in the eighteenth century or earlier. The brick second storey seems to have been added later. This was the home of Billy Judd, the undertaker, who was also chauffeur to the Chinnerys at the

Manor and a carpenter/handyman. Billy was a great village character, who is remembered as a 'loveable rogue' and a great drinker but who could be too clever for his own good! There was nothing mechanical or electrical that he could not fix. He had the first wireless in the village and used to charge up batteries for others. He drove his own Bullnose Morris, one of the first cars in the village. He could be extremely smart, whether dressed as the undertaker or chauffeuring the Chinnerys.

THE YARD was formerly known as PRENTICE YARD, after William Prentice, a butcher from Bicester, who bought it from Thomas Gibbard of Laurels Farm in April 1902 for £310. The group of nine cottages had also been sold as a block in 1875 when it was known as Franklin's Yard. The Yard used to have another row of three or four cottages on the edge of the lane. The first one was a grocery shop, remembered as 'Mrs Carey's', where there used to be a chocolate machine on a post outside the shop. The shop remained open until the row of cottages was demolished when Prentice Yard was split up in the early 1950s.

'Granny Wright' had a small sweetshop in part of what is now STABLE COTTAGE (formerly Samarkand). Behind it there used to be two more cottages. MAVIS HOUSE, which was also part of the group, has now been modernised and extended on the right-hand end.

PUMP COTTAGE is named after the pump, which was used by the residents on Rectory Lane and by the Old School. In 1944, the headteacher, Harold Corfe, commented for the benefit of his successor: 'the pump in the scullery and the water from it not fit to poison pigs. All the drinking water in buckets from village pump – 50 yards.'

VIXEN COTTAGE: note the blocked door and window still visible on the north wall and some alterations to the south wall. There used to be two other small stone cottages on the south side. One of them was occupied by Miss Hitchcock, who ran a small shop. Henry Taylor, of Waterloo Farm, demolished both the cottages after he had bought them along with the two brick cottages next door for £100 each. He apparently needed the stone to build some walls.

BOND'S COTTAGES next door, end on to the Lane, are much altered. They used to be two, one of which was occupied by Albert Jackman, the farrier.

FARRIERS CLOSE, which originally would have been part of the

Green, is the latest development in the village, built at the end of the 1990s. Excavations prior to the development revealed a series of Iron Age and Romano-British boundary ditches. These were overlain by a further series of ditches of the tenth or eleventh century, including a possible domestic enclosure. This phase was superseded in the twelfth century by ridge-and-furrow arable activity. This continued until the second half of the thirteenth century when three stone buildings were constructed. One of these appears to have been a farrier's workshop. It is possible that the buildings formed part of a manorial complex. In the middle of the fourteenth century the buildings appear to have been abandoned and the whole area converted to pasture. This was the period of the Black Death and other plagues, which resulted in large-scale depopulation.[20]

PRINGLE COTTAGE was probably built in the eighteenth century. The south end and the bay window were added in the 1950s and at the same time the north end, which used to be a workshop, was converted. Ernest and Ellen Price used to run the Post Office here from c.1910 to 1949. Ernest also worked as a plumber. There used to be a postbox and later a telephone kiosk by the front gate. Members of the Price family lived here and next door in Rose Cottage from the 1860s. They rented the copse across the road by the Old School House as a garden. Many of the Price family were plumbers, painters, decorators, and general builders / repairmen. By a lucky chance some of their old ledgers survived in the attic of Pringle Cottage. They provide a fascinating record of their customers and work from 1869 until the early 1900s.

ROSE COTTAGE was originally a thatched cottage, probably built in the eighteenth century. During the Second World War Sam Goddard, a schoolmaster who came with the evacuees, lived in one half. Lily Price was living in the other half. She was the infants' teacher in the 1940s, when she was described by the headmaster, Mr Corfe, as having no qualifications and being a bit temperamental. But he also thought that she was a solid worker who does jolly well!

You can now retrace your steps to the Green and back to the Butchers Arms.

Notes

1   Flora Thompson, *Still Glides the Stream*, 125.
2   Letter from Flora Thompson, dated 24 February 1945, quoted by Christine Bloxham, *The World of Flora Thompson,* 155.
3   Letter from Flora Thompson in 1939.
4   Ted and Joan Flaxman, *Cottisford Revisited*, 10.
5   *Lark Rise to Candleford*, 18.
6   *Lark Rise to Candleford*, 88.
7   *Lark Rise to Candleford,* 82.
8   *Lark Rise to Candleford,* 219.
9   Local Preachers meetings minute book 1873-93, Northampton Record Office.
10 *Lark Rise to Candleford,* 212.
11 *Lark Rise to Candleford,* 289.
12 *Country Life*, December 8, 2005, 51.
13 *Lark Rise to Candleford,* 197.
14 *Lark Rise to Candleford,* 177.
15 Oxford Archaeological Unit (OAU) Paper No.6, 2000.
16 *Oxford Chronicle,* 16 Nov.1844.
17 *Lark Rise to Candleford,* 524.
18 J.C. Blomfield, *Fringford* (1890/91), 25.
19 *Bicester Advertiser,* 4 Jan.1901.
20 OAU Paper No.6, 2000.

Bibliography

For those who may wish to explore the history of any of the villages further, I attach a list of the main primary and published sources which I have consulted.

Primary Sources
Census returns 1801-1901
Parish registers
W. Potts, *List and Directory (formerly J.G. Rusher's) 1897-1906*
J.G.Rusher, *Rusher's Banbury's Lists and Directories* (1796-1896)
Trade directories, including *Gardner's, Harrods, Kelly's, and Post Office.*

Published Sources
Pauline Ashbridge, *Village Chapels* (2004).
Joseph Boughey, *Hadfield's British Canals – The Inland Waterways of Britain and Ireland* (1950, fully revised 1994).
Valerie Porter, *English Villagers* (1992).
Valerie Porter, Y*esterday's Countryside, Country Life as it really was* (2000).
The Rotary Club of Bicester, *The Bicester Story – Reflections of Town and Village* (1999).
Jennifer Sherwood & Nikolaus Pevsner, *The Buildings of England: Oxfordshire* (1974).
Jennifer Sherwood, *A Guide to the Churches of Oxfordshire*, (1989).
Kate Tiller, *Church and Chapel in Oxfordshire 1851: The return of the census of religious worship,* Oxfordshire Record Society 55, 1987.
24 Square Miles: film made by the Central Office of Information (1946).
Victoria County History of Oxford, vi (Ploughley Hundred), 1959; ix (Bloxham Hundred), 1969; x (Banbury Hundred), 1972; xi (Wootton Hundred (Northern Part)), 1983.

Chapter 1: Banburyshire: myth or reality?
Ted Clark, *Banbury History and Guide* (1992).
Vera Hodgkins and Christine Bloxham, *Banbury and Shutford Plush* (1980, reprinted 2004).
Brian Little, *Banbury – A History* (2003).
Barrie Trinder, *Victorian Banbury* (1982).

Edwin Walford, The *Pathways of Banburyshire* (1900, reprinted 1983).

Graham Wilton, *The Saxon Princess and Her Infant Saint* (2004).

V. Wood, *The Licensees of the Inns, Taverns and Beerhouses of Banbury, Oxfordshire* (1998).

Raymond B. Wood-Jones, *Traditional Domestic Architecture in the Banbury region* (1963, reprinted 1986).

Chapter 2: Cropredy

Ray Cherry, *Memories of Cropredy* (2005).

Cherwell District Council, *Cropredy Battlefield Walk & Village Trail.* (No.6)

David Clark, *Battlefield Walks – The Midlands* (1993).

Pamela Keegan, *Cropredy – A Village Trail* (undated).

Chapter 3: Fritwell

J.C. Blomfield, *History of the Deanery of Bicester, Part* VII (1893).

M.W. Greenwood, *Parishes, Parsons, and Persuasions: the contrasting clerics and communities of Fringford and Fritwell in 19th-century North Oxfordshire* (1997, not published).

Chapter 4: Lower Heyford

Cherwell District Council, *Cherwell Valley Walks* (No.5).

Peter Deeley, *Valley of the Cherwell: Its People & Places* (2001).

Pamela Horn (ed.), *Oxfordshire Country Life in the 1860s: The early diaries of George James Dew (1846-1928) of Lower Heyford* (1986).

Pamela Horn (ed.), *Oxfordshire Village Life: The Diaries of George James Dew (1846-1928), Relieving Officer* (1983).

Chapter 5: Horley

J.P. Bowes, *Walking Through the Centuries* (1991).

Cherwell District Council, *Horley Circular Walk & Village Trail* (No.10)

Chapter 6: King's Sutton

King's Sutton Parish Council, *Countryside Walks: King's Sutton.*

King's Sutton Village Appraisal Group, *King's Sutton* (1993).

Chapter 7: The Sibfords

Leslie Baily, *From the Romans to Rock-N-Roll: A Short History of the Sibford-Epwell-Hook Norton-District* (1960).

Cherwell District Council, *Sibfords Historic Village Trail* (No.4)
M.R. Finch, *From Manor House to Quaker School* (1997, not published).

Chapter 8: Great Tew
Michael Varney, *Great Tew: Living in the Past* (1991).

Chapter 9: In the Steps of Flora Thompson
J.C. Blomfield, *History of the Deanery of Bicester, Part III* (1887), and *Part V* (1890/91).
Christine Bloxham, *The World of Flora Thompson* (1998).
Ted & Joan Flaxman, *Cottisford Revisited* (1999).
M.W. Greenwood, *Fringford Through the Ages* (2000).
M.W. Greenwood, *Parishes, Parsons and Persuasions* (1997, not published).
Gillian Lindsay, *Flora Thompson: The Story of the 'Lark Rise' Writer* (1990).
Flora Thompson, *Lark Rise to Candleford* (Penguin 1973).
Flora Thompson, *Still Glides the Stream* (1948).

Index